Paul Gochet
Ascent to Truth
A Critical Examination of Quine's Philosophy

Introductiones

Contributions to Philosophical Analysis

Editor:
Hans Burkhardt · Erlangen

Philosophia Verlag München Wien

Paul Gochet

Ascent to Truth
A Critical Examination
of Quine's Philosophy

ERRATUM

p. 82, the first paragraph should be replaced by:

properties. The instantiated feature in virtue of which the same predicate is attributed to different individuals can be construed as an *individual quale.* We have, however, to use appropriate analytic hypotheses and read the syncategorematic expression 'is *F*' as 'contains *F* as a part'.

p. 83, the first line should be replaced by:

(31) For all *a* and all *b*, *a* and *b*, where *a* is referred to before *b*, satisfy '*x* is bigger

Philosophia Verlag München Wien

CIP-Kurztitelaufnahme der Deutschen Bibliothek

Gochet, Paul:
Ascent to Truth. A Critical Examination of Quine's
Philosophy/Paul Gochet – München Wien: Philosophia
Verlag, 1986.
(Introductiones)
ISBN 3-88405-050-8

Published with subsidies from the Förderungs- und Beihilfefonds
Wissenschaft der VG WORT.

ISBN 3-88405-050-8
© 1986 by Philosophia Verlag GmbH., München
All rights reserved. No part of this book may be reproduced
in any manner, by print, photoprint, microfilm, or any other
means without written permission except in the case of
short quotations in the context of reviews.
Typesetting: Königshausen & Neumann, Würzburg
Manufactured by WB-Druck GmbH., Rieden a.F.
Printed in Germany 1986

For Jacques Ruytinx
with gratitude

Table of Contents

Preface 11

Introduction 13

I. The Critique and Revision of Logical Empiricism 15

1. Historical Perspective: Two Fundamental Tenets of Logical Empiricism 15
2. Two Dogmas of Empiricism 16
3. Grice's and Strawson's Reply: an Assessment 21
4. Priest's Rejoinder 26
5. Quine's Epistemological Holism 28
6. Language and Theory 34

II. The Theory of Meaning 39

1. Platonism, Mentalism and Behavioural Semantics 39
2. Radical Translation and Behaviourism 42
3. Stimulus Meaning 43
4. Occasion, Standing, Eternal, Observational and Theoretical Sentences 44
5. The Relation Between Observation Sentences and Holism Revisited 46
6. The Distinction Between Meaning and Collateral Information for Observation Sentences 47
7. The Meaning of Non-Observational Occasion Sentences 48
8. The Limits of Naturalism and of the Experimental Method 50
9. Analytical Hypotheses 51
10. The Indeterminacy of Translation 52
11. A Critique of the Thesis that Translation is Indeterminate 55
12. Inscrutability of Reference 57
13. Indeterminacy of Translation, the Weaker Versus the Stronger Version 61

III. Ontology — 65

1. The Critique of the Linguistic Conception of Ontology — 65
2. The Criterion of Ontological Commitment — 67
3. Is the Predicate 'x is committed to y' Extensional? — 71
4. B. Taylor's Formalization of the Criterion of Ontological Commitment — 73
5. Vuillemin's Objection to the Criterion of Ontological Commitment — 76
6. The Syntactic and Semantic Status of Predicates — 79
7. Quine and the Traditional Problem of Universals, Trapp's Criticism — 83
8. Has Quine Two Ontologies? — 85
9. Ontology, Ideology and Ontological Commitment — 90
10. Proxy Functions — 92
11. Ontological Relativity — 95

IV. Epistemology — 100

1. The Abandonment of Foundationalism — 100
2. From Rational to Genetic Reconstruction of Concepts — 102
3. An Alternative to Doctrinal Foundationalism — 105
4. The Scope and the Limits of Epistemology Naturalized — 106
5. Immanent Versus Transcendent Epistemology — 107
6. Ontological Relativity and Transcendental Questions — 110
7. The Immanence of Truth and the Disappearence of Transcendent Questions — 111
8. Difficulties Arising from the Concept of Truth as Immanent to Theories — 113
9. The Originality of TUD — 114
10. The Threat of Relativism Generated by TUD — 119
11. An Assessment of TUD — 124

V. The Demarcation of Logic — 126

1. Logical Truths and Analyticity — 126
2. Steps Towards a Definition of the Notion of Logical Particle — 129
3. Logical Form and Grammatical Structure — 130
4. Recurrence and Synonymy — 135
5. Relations Between Logical Truths and Language — 137
6. Model-Theoretic Versus Proof-Theoretic Conceptions of Logic — 138

VI. Deviant Logics — 141

1. Quine's Oscillations Between Conservatism and Liberalism in Logic — 141
2. Against the Incommensurability Thesis — 142
3. For and Against Revisionism in Logic — 145
4. Verdict Functions Versus Truth-Functions — 147

VII. Quantified Modal Logic — 150

1. From Intensionality to Referential Opacity — 150
2. From the Slingshot Argument to Essentialism — 154
3. On Essentialism — 157
4. On Genuine Singular Terms — 160
5. Identification of Individuals Across Possible Worlds — 160
6. Propositional Attitudes — 164
7. What is Left After the Elimination of the *de re* Construction? — 168

Conclusion — 171

Bibliography — 175

Index of Names — 191

Index of Subjects — 195

Preface

It would not have been possible for me to complete this work had I not been awarded a one year Fellowship by the American Council of Learned Societies, and later on a Fellowship at the Australian National University. I should like to extend my grateful thanks to them both. Amongst other things, my Fellowships enabled me to meet Professor Quine in Harvard and Professor J.J.C. Smart in Canberra. I should like to thank them both for the encouragement they gave me, and the time they devoted to discussing the main theses of this book. I want also to express my gratitude to Professor David Holdcroft for performing the unrewarding task of translating my manuscript and to Professor Susan Haack who made thorough comments on the whole manuscript. The book owes much to them, not only stylistically, but also philosophically. They pointed out to me the various weaknesses of the first draft. Those which remain should be imputed to me alone. The written comments by Sir Alfred Ayer, Tyler Burge, Henri Lauener, Albert Menne, Julius Moravcsik and Avrum Stroll and the suggestions made by Dr. Hausser and the editor Dr. Dr. Hans Burkhardt have enabled me to make many improvements in the final draft. I benefited greatly from criticisms made by various audiences to which parts of this book were submitted: the philosophical seminars at several Australian Universities (Canberra, Melbourne, La Trobe, Monash, Macquarie) and Dutch Universities (Amsterdam, Groningen). I also had access to unpublished works which were of great assistance to me while writing this book: Dr. Barry Taylor's M.A. dissertation, Dr. Michael McRobbie's Ph. D. dissertation, Dr. Allen Hazen's Ph. D. dissertation, Dr. Richard Routley's preprints to mention but a few. Last but not least I express my deep gratitude to the Förderungs- und Beihilfefonds Wissenschaft der VG Wort GmbH., München.

Bibliographical convention: The date given after the author's name indicates when the paper referred to was published for the first time. The page numbers which follow refer to a later publication, in cases where the article has been reprinted in an anthology as mentioned in the bibliography.

Introduction

Several important monographs dealing with Quine's philosophy have come out recently. W.K. Essler's "Quine: Empirismus auf pragmatischer Grundlage" (1975); Professor Orenstein's book *Willard Van Orman Quine* (1977) and Professor J. Largeault's *Quine, Questions de mots, Questions de faits* (1980). In 1982 Professor Lauener published a monograph in German which Quine describes as a "masterly presentation, clear and appreciative of [his] point of view" and this is all the more striking since he is not a Quinean – he describes himself as an 'open transcendentalist'. To that extent his monograph can be set off against Professor Gibson's book which aims at offering to the reader both an exposition and a vindication of Quine's position. Quine warmly approved of this monograph which gives him, as he says, a "welcome perspective on [his] own work".

Last but not least, in 1983, George Romanos published an essay whose title "Quine and Analytic Philosophy. The Language of Language" neatly brings out what makes the book a useful addition to the literature on Quine's philosophy. As Quine again notes, "the book is rich in historical background, perceptively interpreted and interrelated".

I shall not attempt to compete with my predecessors and will adopt a different perspective. Everyone agrees that Quine's essays have changed the philosophical scene and, as Romanos puts it, that philosophy will never be the same. Yet Quine's views have been persistently challenged. His allegedly devastating criticism of modal logic, just to mention one example, sowed the seeds for a rich harvest of sophisticated replies and arguments.

It is the purpose of my monograph to assess the cogency of these arguments and to isolate what is of lasting value in Quine's position.

I will not restrict myself to the role of an umpire. Rather, I will enter the arena and offer positive or negative criticism of my own. As I share Quine's general standpoint, i.e. his relative empiricism, my criticism will be *mainly internal criticism*: it will consist in pointing out the stresses, strains and inner tensions which reveal themselves as soon as one tries to put together Quine's sundry doctrines and positions.

I will also try to restore unity and consistency wherever they are in danger, either by developing Quine's insights further or by proposing new solutions.

Rather than deal with the whole work, I will focus on a few central themes in Quine's philosophy and try to treat them thoroughly[1].

---

[1] The questions examined in this monograph significantly differ from those treated in my *Quine en perspective* (Paris, Flammarion, 1978) translated into German by P. Bosch (*Quine zur Diskussion*) (Berlin, Ullstein, 1984). I tried to avoid overlap as much as I could.

I
The Critique and Revision of Logical Empiricism

1. Historical Perspective: Two Fundamental Tenets of Logical Empiricism

Amongst the epistemological theses defended by the Vienna Circle there are two which occupy a central position. The first of these, the Verification Principle, states that a proposition has a meaning if, and only if, it is empirically verifiable. This principle embodies an extreme version of Empiricism, for not only is sense-experience invoked as the source of *knowledge*, but also as a condition of *meaningfulness*. The second thesis is the doctrine that logical truths are linguistic in nature, in that they are true solely in virtue of the meanings of the logical words that they contain. Moreover, the Logical Positivists maintained that the class of propositions true solely in virtue of the meanings of the *logical* words they contain is but a sub-class of a much larger class of propositions true solely in virtue of the meanings of any words they contain, be they logical such as 'not', 'and', and 'all', or non-logical such as 'bachelor', 'green', etc. As for mathematics, either it was thought that is was reducible to logic, in the manner of the logicist programme of Russell and Whitehead, or else, following Hilbert, it was thought of as an uninterpreted formalism.

Metaphysicians have usually acknowledged that the statements of metaphysics are not verifiable by sense-experience. Instead, many of them have invoked a source of knowledge that is *sui generis*, intellectual intuition for instance. Moreover, they have refused to assimilate metaphysical statements to analytic statements lacking factual content, often claiming that the former have the status of synthetic *a priori* truths. It follows, therefore, that anyone who subscribes to the two central theses of Logical Positivism mentioned above ought to reject metaphysics conceived of in this way, not merely because it is concerned with a domain about which we must remain forever ignorant, but more *radically* because it is a 'domain' about which one cannot say anything meaningful.

Thus, deprived of one of its major domains by the elimination of metaphysics, philosophy had to change its conception of its object and status. It would no longer be a branch of knowledge parallel with science, but a second level discourse, that is, a discourse about scientific discourse. The first step toward this transformation of philosophy is already clearly taken by Wittgenstein in the *Tractatus Logico-Philosophicus*:

> The correct method in philosophy would really be the following: to say nothing except what can be said, i.e. propositions of natural science – i.e. something that has nothing to do with philosophy – and then, whenever someone else wanted to say something metaphysical, to demonstrate to him that he had failed to give a meaning to certain signs in his propositions. (Wittgenstein [1921], 6.53)

As early as 1951, in his epoch making paper "Two Dogmas of Empiricism", Quine frontally attacked the second of the two central theses of the Vienna Circle mentioned at the beginning. On the other hand, he affirmed his commitment to a version, admittedly an amended one, of the Verification Theory of Meaning. This commitment to Empiricism, moreover, lends great weight to his critique; for it is an *internal* critique of a sympathizer, rather than an *external* one from an adversary. By attacking one of the two pillars on which the anti-metaphysical arguments of the Logical Positivists and the Linguistic Analysts rested, Quine reopened the problem of the legitimacy of metaphysics which had been thought to be solved. For he did not confine himself to criticizing the doctrine that logical truths are linguistic in nature, he proposed an alternative doctrine. Now this doctrine carried along in its wake a rehabilitation of metaphysics, though of a metaphysics which henceforth would be *continuous* with, and not external to, natural science, and hence both immune from the critique of the Positivists, and compatible with it.

It can thus be seen that the issues raised by Quine's argument in "Two Dogmas of Empiricism" are immense. It even brings into question again the status of philosophy itself. For this reason we have chosen to approach Quine's work through a study of this paper, even though it is not his first important philosophical paper. We shall then consider the reply by Grice and Strawson that it prompted; concluding with an attempt to adjudicate between them.

2. Two Dogmas of Empiricism

Quine's paper begins with an extremely clear statement of intention. There are two theses espoused by modern Empiricism that he disputes: (i) the claim that there is "... some fundamental cleavage between truths which are *analytic*, or grounded in meanings independently of matters of fact, and truths which are *synthetic*, or grounded in fact" ([1951a], p. 20). And (ii) the claim that "... each meaningful statement is equivalent to some logical construct upon terms which refer to immediate experience" ([1951a], p. 20); a claim which implies that the empirical information of a theory can be distributed over separate sentences.

Quine's strategy consists of reviewing the various definitions of *analyticity* that have been proposed, submitting them to criticism one by one. Now in the class of analytic truths which are allegedly grounded in meaning alone, it is possible to distinguish a subclass, that of logical truths, typified by

(1) No unmarried man is married.

For these it is possible to adopt a definition which is non-committal on the question of the linguistic nature of logical truths. This definition, originated by Bolzano, was revived by Quine who states it thus:

If we suppose a prior inventory of *logical* particles, comprising 'no', 'un-', 'not', 'if', 'then', 'and', etc., then in general a logical truth is a statement which is true and remains true under all reinterpretations of its components other than the logical particles ([1951a], p. 22–23).

Given this definition it seems, at first sight, extremely easy to define the class of non-logical analytic truths typified by

(2) No bachelor is married.

For "The characteristic of such a statement is that it can be turned into a logical truth by putting synonyms for synonyms; thus (2) can be turned into (1) by putting 'unmarried man' for its synonym 'bachelor'" (Quine [1951a], p. 23).

However, this definition uses the term 'synonymous' which in turn needs to be explained. The first suggestion that comes to mind is that two linguistic forms are synonymous if, and only if, they are interchangeable *salva veritate* in all contexts. But what must be understood by the expression 'all contexts'? If one includes amongst them contexts involving quotation, one will be forced to treat as non-synonymous the expressions 'quadrilateral' and 'figure with four sides', since they are not interchangeable *salva veritate* in

(3) '..............' has less than fourteen letters.

If, on the other hand, one included only extensional contexts, that is modes of containment whose extension (truth-value, extension, reference) is a unique function of the extensions of its constituents, one will have to class as synonyms the expressions 'creature with a heart' and 'creature with kidneys'. But this manoeuvre amounts to confusing co-extensivity with synonymity.

In order to avoid these two pitfalls, one must make precise what 'all contexts' means in a way which excludes contexts involving quotation, but includes intensional contexts constructed using modal adverbs, such as 'necessarily'. For an intensional language, that is an extensional language L to which has been added the adverb 'necessarily' (L $\cup$ {'necessarily'})[1], enables one to construct contexts which distinguish expressions that are synonymous with each other from ones that are merely coextensive. Thus, if in the context

(4) Necessarily all and only A's are A

one has substituted for the two occurrences of A two occurrences of any grammatically admissible expression, the replacement of one of these occurrences by an expression that is merely coextensive will not preserve truth value, as is shown by the passage from (5) to (6) below:

(5) Necessarily all cordates are cordates

(6) Necessarily all cordates are renates.

On the other hand, substitution of an expression which our linguistic competence leads us to class as synonymous would preserve truth value. One might, therefore, be tempted to conclude that interchangeability *salva veritate* in the language (L $\cup$ {'necessarily'}) is a good test of synonymy. Unfortunately, the term 'necessarily' now, in its turn, demands to be

---

[1] i.e. the union of the set of the well-formed formulas of the extensional language and of the set of formulas obtained by prefixing sentences with the adverb 'necessarily'.

explicated. But if we now ask Carnap ([1934], p. 304), for example, to explain the object language expression

(7) An object c necessarily possesses the property P,

he would reply by translating it into an expression of the syntactical metalanguage thus,

(8) '$P(c)$' is analytic.

At this point the attempt to define analyticity shipwrecks, for the proposed definition is evidently circular.

The situation is not improved if one gives oneself in addition the resources of formal semantics. Doubtless one could construct an artificial language L_0 furnished with semantic rules, even with a tool that Carnap's formal semantics lacked when Quine wrote "Two Dogmas of Empiricism", namely, meaning postulates (Carnap [1956], p. 222–229). Having done this one could say that a statement is analytic in L_0 if, and only if, it is true in virtue of the semantic rules and postulates of L_0. For example, if L_0 is an interpreted first order calculus containing both the name 'Albert' and the meaning postulate

(9) $(\forall x)\,(x$ is a bachelor $\supset x$ is not-married$)$[1]

one could establish that

(10) If Albert is a bachelor, then Albert is not married

is analytic-in-L_0.

Unfortunately, this strategy enables one only to define 'analytic-in-L_0', 'analytic-in-L_1', etc, but not analyticity in general, that is 'analytic-in-L' where 'L' is a variable and not a constant. For to date no one has succeeded in giving a non-arbitrary list of meaning postulates that are common to all languages, and hence which would belong to a universal artificial language. This second attempt to define analyticity has, therefore, failed like the first, but for a different reason: the definition proposed is not circular, but arbitrary.

---

[1] i.e. for all x, if x is a bachelor, x is not married.

The third and final attempt to define analyticity rests on either a consequence, or an attenuated form, of the second dogma of empiricism, that is, the thesis that the empirical information of a theory can be distributed over separate sentences. If this thesis is admitted, one can define synonymy: "Statement synonymy is said to be likeness of method of empirical confirmation or infirmation" (Quine [1951a], p. 38). One could then define a partial ordering on statements on the basis of their empirical content: (a) certain statements will be confirmed (infirmed) by a single empirical observation, (b) others by several observations, and (c) others will be confirmed (infirmed) 'come what may'. Thus the following statements (11), (12) and (13) are examples respectively of (a), (b) and (c).

(11)   It is raining at time t_0 at place p_0.

(12)   It is raining, or it is snowing, or the wind is blowing, or ... at time t_0 at place p_0.

(13)   Either it is raining or it is not at time t_0 at place p_0.

In other words, according to this third definition, an analytic statement is one that is vacuously confirmed. What is there to complain about in such a definition?

Obviously, the definition 'saves' analyticity by relying on an attenuated form of the dogma of reductionism, i.e. on the view according to which "... each statement, taken in isolation from its fellows, can admit of confirmation or infirmation at all" (Quine [1951a], p. 41). Thus, Quine argues that

> ... the one dogma clearly supports the other in this way: as long as it is taken to be significant in general to speak of the confirmation and infirmation of a statement, it seems significant to speak also of a limiting kind of statement which is vacuously confirmed, *ipso facto*, come what may; and such a statement is analytic. ([1951a], p. 41)

But if it is true that reductionism supports the analytic-synthetic distinction, then the refutation of reductionism will at best leave the dichotomy in the position of an *unsupported dogma*. To suppose it did more than this would be to commit an elementary logical fallacy. The bearing of Quine's argument at this point is clear: the refutation of reductionism is not a refutation of the analytic-synthetic distinction. It merely shifts the burden of proof. Admittedly, Quine also made the stronger claim that "the two dogmas are, indeed, at root identical" ([1951a], p. 41) but this can hardly be reconciled with the claim that they *support* each other unless we are prepared to commit the fallacy of begging the question. Moreover Priest has argued, conclusively in my opinion, that it is possible to maintain one without the other (Priest [1979], p. 293). Before stating his arguments, however, I shall review one of the most famous vindications of the analytic-synthetic dichotomy: Grice's and Strawson's "In Defence of a Dogma".

3. Grice's and Strawson's Reply: an Assessment

Central to their rejoinder is a criticism of Quine's method. They concede that his criticisms of the various definitions of analyticity are not without foundation, but maintain that the fact that philosophers have failed to conceptualize a distinction does not prove that there is not one to be made. It is one thing to be able to *apply* a distinction; quite another to be able to *define* it. For

... those who use the terms "analytic" and "synthetic" do to a very considerable extent agree in the applications they make of them ... This agreement extends not only to cases which they have been *taught* so to characterize, but to new cases. (Grice and Strawson [1956], p. 83)

The fact pointed out by Grice and Strawson is indisputable, but the interpretation given of it by them is not compelling. For the existence of the fact in question would not support the analytic-synthetic distinction, if it were possible to accommodate it in a theory compatible with Quine's position. Dr. B. Cohen has recently developed such a theory. He begins by introducing the notion of a prototype:

... a prototype for a concept K is a mental representation consisting of a set of weighted non-necessary features F_i that provide a *probabilistic summary* of the properties of the corresponding category K. (B. Cohen [1982], p. 65)

For example, 'flies' is a trait figuring in the prototype of 'bird', but the connection between 'bird' and 'flies' is not definitional. Prototypes license what are called '*default* inferences', that is "... inferences which are 'valid' *so long as there is no evidence* to the contrary" (Cohen [1982], p. 83).

Default inferences violate the *monotonicity principle* of standard logic: adding new premises, (further evidence) may require one to cancel inferences previously made by default.

Let us return now to an earlier example in which the concept 'bachelor' is construed as a prototype,

(14) All bachelors are unmarried.

Cohen sees (14) not as an analytic statement, but as a *typicality judgment* which, he suggests, can be formalized, with the aid of the typicality-operator '∇', as follows:

(15) $(\forall x) (\nabla \text{ Bachelor } (x) \supset \text{unmarried } (x))$

which literally is read as,

(16) All typical bachelors are unmarried.

Typicality judgments are not to be confused with traditional analytic judgments: "Typicality judgements have been found to depend on a variety of other forms of knowledge [other than 'linguistic' knowledge] including frequency information, correlational information, and functional knowledge." (Cohen [1982], p. 123–124)

However, though we have so far shown that there is an interpretation of the facts that rivals that of Grice and Strawson, we have still not shown that it is superior. To this end, the divergent views of Grice and Strawson, on the one hand, and Cohen, on the other, can be summarized and compared thus:

Grice's and Strawson's account

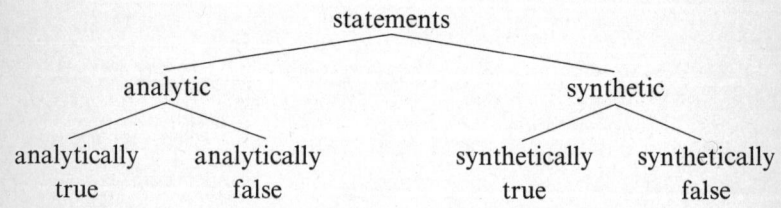

Cohen's account

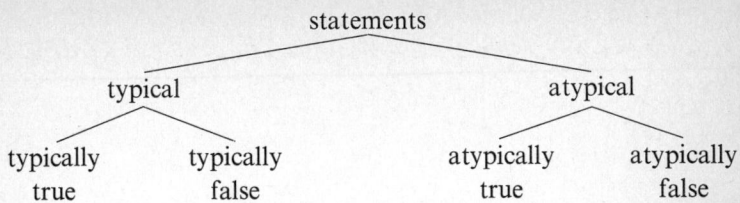

To decide between the two classifications, one can imagine the following crucial experiment: if a statement classed as *analytically false* is, in fact, only a statement that is *typically false*, the use of an operator 'suspending' the typicality operator – what Cohen calls a *hedge* – should now place it in the category of atypical statements, which contains the statements classed as synthetic by Grice and Strawson. If, on the other hand, they are really analytic, then the suspension-operator should have no effect on their analyticity. At first sight, the experimental data seem to support Quine and Cohen and undermine Grice's and Strawson's account. Consider the following example which we borrow from Cohen:

(17)   Jane is a female bachelor.

In so far as one is restricted to considering only (17), it is right to hesitate between the alternative descriptions of it as 'typically false' and 'analytically false'. However, let us introduce the suspending operator 'a sort of', so that we can consider additionally:

(18)   Jane is a sort of female bachelor.

Now, as Cohen argues,

> Though judgments may vary, to the liberated mind ... 'Jane is sort of a female bachelor' ... may well be true, implying something of cognitive import about Jane's life style and marital status, for example, that Jane lives the life style of a bachelor. ([1982], p. 103, 104)

Indeed French has even lexicalized the phenomenon:

(19)   Jeanne est une garçonne.

Can we say that a woman who has the life style of a bachelor is 'a sort of bachelor', i.e. a bachelor but an a-typical one and deny analyticity to 'bachelors are male'? Cohen seems to ignore an important distinction here.

Even if it is true that the statements

(20)   Helicopters have *some sort* of wings

(21)   Some bachelors are *somehow* married

are more acceptable than

(22)   Helicopters have wings

(23)   Some bachelors are married

it is not at all for the same reason. The 'hedge' (*some sort, somehow*) plays a different role in the two statements. In (20), the propeller is viewed as a wing, although an a-typical one, on the basis of a functional equivalence which exists between the propeller of a helicopter and the wings of a plane. In balloons, hydrogen is what maintains the vessel above the ground, but there are not enough functional similarities between balloons and planes for us to say that hydrogen is functionally equivalent to a wing. Hence hydrogen does not qualify as a wing, not even as a *sort* of wing. In (21), the bachelors who live the style of life of married men are described as 'married'. But with respect to the law they are not married at all. The use of the word 'somehow' triggers a *figurative* or *metaphorical* reading of the word 'married'. It changes the *meaning* of the word and in this respect it shows that initially the statement was false *ex vi terminorum*. A statement is analytically false when to make it true, we have to change the meaning of some word contained in it rather than the world.

I conclude that Cohen's interesting findings, although they show that some allegedly analytic statements are not analytic after all, do not succedd in establishing that the analytic-synthetic distinction is a distinction without a difference.

For a new approach see Zuber, R. "Analyticity and Genericness" (Zuber [1978]).

Let us now turn back to "In Defence of a Dogma". Interestingly, Grice and Strawson refuse to allow that the notion of synonymy is as uncertain as that of analyticity. For the former is not a technical notion belonging to philosophy, as is the latter. Rejection of the ordinary notion of synonymity would have paradoxical consequences. To give up the opposition 'synonymous' *versus* 'non-synonymous', would, they maintain, be to renounce the distinction between 'correct' and 'incorrect translation': "Is all talk of correct or incorrect *translation* of sentences of one language into sentences of another meaningless? It is hard to believe that it is." (Grice and Strawson [1956], p. 85)

However Quine had both anticipated this objection, and replied to it, (in 1954), in "Carnap and Logical Truth" which appeared only in 1960 – four years after the paper by Grice and Strawson. Quine recognized that when we are confronted with an ethnologist who proposes to translate the native's sentence

(24)　q Ka bu q,

by

(25)　p and not p,

we seem to have a choice between two responses: either to impute, as did Lévy-Bruhl a prelogical mentality to the natives, or to impute, as would Lévi-Strauss in such a case, a bad translation to the ethnologist. Quine, however, questioned the objective nature of the disjunction.

> ... illogical cultures are indistinguishable from ill-translated ones ...
> For, there can be ... no stronger evidence ... of bad translation than that it translates earnest affirmations into obvious falsehoods (Quine [1960b], pp. 112–113).

For the qualitative opposition (linguistic truth *versus* factual truth) Quine substitutes a quantitative opposition (more obvious *versus* less obvious). The example of (25) shows that Quine does not limit himself to rejecting the arguments for the isolation of analytic statements (true or false) which are not logical statements as a separate class, but also does the same for logical statements. It is the very doctrine of the linguistic nature of logical truth that is brought into question. We shall return to this point in Chapter Five.

Surprisingly, Grice and Strawson are not disturbed by the impossibility of citing a single example of an unrevisable principle, i.e., one true 'come what may'. They concede to Quine that "... there is no absolute necessity about the adoption or use of any conceptual scheme whatever ..." (Grice and Strawson [1956], p. 93).

... it is one thing to admit this, and quite another thing to say that there are no necessities within any conceptual scheme we adopt or use, or, more narrowly again, that there are no linguistic forms which do express analytic propositions. (Grice and Strawson [1956], p. 93)

In formal terms, they reject the following, in which 'p' ranges over sentences and 'S' over conceptual schemes,

(26) $(\exists p)(\forall S)(p$ is analytic in $S)$ [1]

but they accept,

(27) $(\forall S)(\exists p)(p$ is analytic in $S)$ [2].

Grice and Strawson succeed, therefore, in reconciling the analytic-synthetic distinction with the absence of any statements that are irrevisably true 'come what may'.

But it is one thing to show that the analytic-synthetic dichotomy is *consistent* with there being no unrevisable statement, and quite another thing to offer an argument which *supports* the dichotomy.

Quine is sceptical about the possibility of working out such an argument. He is ready to concede that there are no better grounds for choosing rejection of the dichotomy rather than the opposing views: "My misgivings over the notion of analyticity are ... misgivings in principle. But those also who espouse the notion espouse it mainly in principle" (Quine [1953a] p. 139). Yet it should not be concluded that the dispute has reached a stalemate. Priest has put forward an argument supporting the claim that we have good reasons to espouse *in principle* the analytic-synthetic dichotomy.

4. Priest's Rejoinder

In a well known argument, Lewis Caroll has shown that if we transform all rules of inference into axioms, we generate a *regressio ad infinitum*, we deprive ourselves of the dynamic factor which enabled us to *move* from the

---

[1] There is a sentence p such that, for all conceptual schemes S, p is analytic in S.
[2] For all conceptual schemes S, there is a sentence p such that p is analytic in S.

premisses to the conclusion. To break the regress we have to make a sharp *distinction* between statements on the one hand and rules of inference on the other. Next we can isolate conditionals *corresponding* to rules.

For instance, the conditional "If it is the case that p and that if p then q, then q" corresponds to the rule of *modus ponens* "From 'If p then q' and 'p' deduce 'q'". If we say that these conditionals are analytic we have a sharp distinction, as sharp as the one between rules of inference and statements, or between structure and content. Yet we still do not have a fully satisfactory definition. We want more. We want the class of analytic statements to be *closed under deduction*. This is why Priest improves on the first definition and writes:

I propose the following characterization of analyticity: an analytic sentence is any sentence which can be validly inferred from conditionals corresponding to valid rules of inference... (Priest [1979], p. 292)

Priest's definition reminds us of the definition of analytic truth, which makes reference to *semantic rules*. Quine objects to the latter definition on the grounds that the distinction between semantical rule and factual truth is *arbitrary*: a semantical rule is distinguishable "only by the fact of appearing on a page under the heading 'Semantical Rules'" (Quine quoted by Priest [1979], p. 293). But Priest operates with *logical* rules instead.

Are logical rules – i.e. rules of inference – better off than semantical rules? Priest claims that they are. He contends that they enjoy as good a theoretical status as *grammatical rules*.

Are the grammatical rules of a natural language solely those rules to be found in a grammar book on a page under the heading 'Grammatical Rules'? Clearly not. (Priest [1979], p. 294)

It is clear that the distinction between well formed and ill formed sentences is better entrenched than the distinction between definitions and factual statements.

A good grammar should systematize and predict the judgments of well-formedness and of ill-formedness that native speakers give on particular sentences of natural language. In the same manner, a good logic should systematize and predict the judgments of validity and invalidity that reasoners have already.

Admittedly Priest subscribes to a Wittgensteinian account of validity which Quine would reject. "A rule is valid if and only if it is ... one of the standards which govern people's practice of inferring." (Priest [1979], p. 269)

To that extent he is offering an alternative rather than an objection to Quine's account of validity. If one sticks to Quine's model-theoretic view of validity, i.e. to the view that validity is the property of rules which are truth preserving (for all interpretations of the non-logical symbols in the sentences connected by the rules of inference), then a definition of analyticity along Priest's lines will fail to include some paradigm positivist examples of analytical sentences. It will include logical truths such as 'All bachelors are bachelors', but exclude 'All bachelors are unmarried'.[1]

Even if one sides with Quine and takes up the standard conception of validity, there is an important lesson to be learned from Lewis Carroll and Priest, namely that rules of inference – and analytical sentences (at least the logical truths among them) do not belong on the same *level* as factual statements. With respect to the 'web of belief', they enjoy an *autonomy* to which Quine does not do full justice when he merely grants them the privilege of lying in the center of the web of belief. Priest's elaboration of Lewis Carroll's insight strikes a blow to Quine's *gradualism* and supports the dichotomy between logical truths and factual truths. We shall say more about this in Chapter VI (p. 146).

As to the second dogma, Priest agrees with Quine's generalized holism: everything is revisable, "... both structure and content may be changed" and joins Grice and Strawson in disassociating the two dogmas which Quine claimed to be at root identical.

5. Quine's Epistemological Holism

In *La théorie physique, son objet, sa structure*, Duhem writes:

To try to separate each of the hypotheses of theoretical physics from the other suppositions on which this science rests, in order to submit it in isolation to the test of experience is to pursue a chimera ... The only experimental test of the physical theory that is not illogical consists in comparing the entire system of physical theory with the whole set of experimental laws ... (Duhem [1914], p. 284)

---

[1] On this topic see Calloway [1982].

Duhem's doctrine, which we will call 'restricted epistemological holism' is, however, limited to physics. Duhem explicitly admits the existence of crucial experiments in physiology. It does not make sense to speak of the verification of isolated statements in physics, but it does in other sciences. One could, therefore, quite coherently subscribe to Duhem's version of holism and, at the same time, maintain that some isolated statements are true in virtue of an observable fact whilst others are true come what may, and hence are analytic. Indeed, Carnap is a case in point since he espoused both Duhem's thesis and the analytic-synthetic dichotomy in the *Logical Syntax of Language*. (Carnap [1937], p. 318)

Quine's holism, by comparison, covers a much wider domain: it embraces the whole of science and, indeed, all knowledge

> The totality of our so-called knowledge or beliefs, from the most casual matters of geography and history to the profoundest laws of atomic physics or even of pure mathematics and logic, is a man-made fabric which impinges on experience only along the edges. Or, to change the figure, total science is like a field of force whose boundary conditions are experience. (Quine [1951a], p. 42)

Duhem's holism rests on the fact that when there is a conflict between theory and observation there are several ways of amending the theory: "... when experience is in conflict with his [the physicist's] predictions, it teaches him that at least one of the hypotheses constituting this set is unacceptable and should be changed, but does not tell him which should be changed" (Duhem [1914], p. 284). Thus Duhem allows that if there is a conflict between an observation statement O and a theory H_1, one would have a choice between replacement theories $H_2 \vee H_3, \ldots \vee H_n$; but he did not envisage that one could even revise O itself. But, Quine's holism goes further: "Even a statement very close to the periphery can be held true in the face of recalcitrant experience by pleading hallucination ..." (Quine [1951a], p. 43)

To preserve a law one can, therefore, on Quine's account *disqualify an observation*. To save a law one can even *change the meanings* of words. Quine is well aware of the paradoxical character of the latter claim and has explained why he made it:

> I haven't advanced it as an interesting thesis as such. I bring it in only in the course of arguing against such notions as that the empirical content of sentences can in general be sorted out distributively, sentence by sentence, or that the understanding of a term can be segregated from collateral information regarding the object. For such

purposes I am not concerned even to avoid the trivial extreme of sustaining a law by changing a meaning ... (Quine [1963b], p. 132)

Quine's holism has been criticized on many grounds, of which we shall examine three: (a) it is too loosely defined; (b) it is too sweeping; and (c) it is inconsistent with the geometrical metaphor which likens knowledge to a circle with a centre and a periphery.

(a) If one accepts that a law can be preserved by changing the meanings of words, one runs the risk of collapsing *holism* into *conventionalism*. More precisely, one risks obliterating the distinction that exists between Duhem's holism and Poincaré's conventionalism. And in Grünbaum's view, this is a valuable distinction which it is important to safeguard.

The difference between the two positions can be illustrated as follows. Imagine that a physicist of the Duhemian school and a disciple of Poincaré both maintain that it is always possible to save a certain geometry, Euclidean geometry, for instance; despite this agreement they will, nevertheless, differ from each other over the type of argument to which they have recourse. To obtain a physical geometry one gives a physical interpretation to the theoretical terms of an axiomatized pure geometry, terms such as 'congruent', 'length', and 'distance'. The Duhemian physicist will observe that this interpretation "is provided here *through the mediation of hypotheses and laws* which are *collateral* to the geometric theory whose physical meaning is being specified". (Grünbaum [1960], p. 121)

Congruence, for example will be defined by the transportation of rigid measuring rods, which undergo a *theoretical correction* meant to eliminate certain pertubational influences, such as the deformations that the rods can undergo in a non-homogeneous thermal or electromagnetic field. Arguing, as he does, that thermodynamics is necessary to fix the sense of the concept of congruence, the Duhemian physicist will claim with Einstein that "the very logic of computing these corrections precludes that the geometry itself be accessible to experimental ascertainment *in isolation from* other physical regularities". (Grünbaum [1960], p. 120)

According to Grünbaum, a physicist who is a conventionalist, in the way in which Poincaré is, will allow himself much more freedom of manoeuvre than the Duhemian physicist. As well as the right to choose between a development of physical geometry and one of thermodynamics, he will give himself the freedom to adopt a new *metric* in which the length of a rod will vary with its position and orientation in a manner that is not constant. Now, to alter the *metric* to save physical geometry is not only to give oneself the right to make changes in empirical science, it is also to give oneself the right to make changes in ones *semantics* and to initiate *redefinitions*. Hence Quine's extreme holism collapses into conventionalism.

(b) The second criticism has been formulated by J. Vuillemin:

> It is ... an empirical fact that Nature, even if she is not compartmentalized, admits degrees of compartmentalisation. I mean by "compartments" the existence of quasi-closed and self-contained systems, independent to a good approximation from any external intrusion. Science was made possible, as the history of taxonomy, astronomy, statics and dynamics shows, because some such compartments were frequent and elementary enough – inasmuch as they contained few constants and variables tied by linear or at most by quadratic relations – to become an easy object of theoretical reconstruction. (Vuillemin [1979], p. 89)

Vuillemin's criticism brings to the fore an inner tension in Quine's philosophy; a tension between his *empiricism* and his *realism*. This tension will recur again and again.

(c) The third criticism, due to Dummett, brings to the fore yet another tension internal to Quine's philosophy, that between *holism* and *empiricism*. What Dummett criticizes is not exactly holism, but the conjunction of holism with the metaphorical assertion that a statement at the periphery of a theory which is in conflict with experience can be saved, provided that there is an adjustment in the interior of the theory.

This conjunction is described by Dummett as an *explosive mixture*. For the second thesis, in his opinion, leads to the *subversion of the whole metaphor of periphery and interior*. Dummett argues as follows:

> If alternative revisions are always possible, and, in particular, ones which leave the periphery intact, there is no content to saying that the total theory makes contact with experience only at the periphery. Rather, the total theory confronts experience *as a whole*: as a whole, revision is or is not required in it by the occurrence of an experience; but there is not any one point or region in the total theory where the impact is made. The periphery was defined as the set of sentences on which experience directly impinges, the interior as the set of sentences which can receive an impulse from without only when it is transmitted from the periphery via the sentences lying en route. If the system confronts experience only as a whole, then there is no periphery and no interior. (Dummett [1973], p. 593–594)

Dummett tries here to impale Quine on the horns of a dilemma: he ought either to abandon *holism*, or abandon *empiricism* that assigns a privileged position to observation sentences.

Quine, however, rejects both of the alternatives presented by Dummett's dilemma. He does, indeed, reject the idea of a *difference in kind* between observation sentences – the periphery – and other statements, but he continues to accord a privileged epistemological status to observation sentences as such. For him, *all* statements, whether they are located at the periphery or not, are *vulnerable*, but they do not all have the same *degree* of vulnerability:

Now the Duhem thesis still holds, in a somewhat literalistic way, even for these observation statements. For the scientist does occasionally revoke even an observation statement, when it conflicts with a well attested body of theory and when he has tried in vain to reproduce the experiment, But the Duhem thesis would be wrong if understood as imposing an equal status on all the statements in a scientific theory and thus denying the strong presumption in favor of the observation statements. It is this bias that makes science empirical. (Quine [1975b], p. 314)

It might be retorted that to be able to attribute a privileged epistemological status to observation sentences – even if it is only one that is relative, it is necessary first to *identify* them. But holism seems to put at risk the very idea of a distinct *class* of observation sentences to the extent that it makes the difference between *observation sentences* and *theoretical sentences* one of degree, and not one of kind. The evident conflict between the two metaphors used by Quine brings the following difficulty into the open: if science is like a field of force, as the second metaphor suggests, how can one still speak of the interior and the exterior, or of the centre and the periphery of the total theory?

This is indeed a serious problem. If we subscribe to a full blooded holism, we have to admit that every sentence is *to a certain extent* theory-laden. It looks as though we have to give up talking of a 'tribunal of experience', i.e., give up *Empiricism*.

If we adopt the standard account of observation sentences, i.e., if we take them to be compounds made out of words which are syntactically related, then Dummett's dilemma is fatal to Quine, for in that case observation sentences are an ill-defined set. They cannot neatly be separated from typically theoretical sentences. There are two reasons why this separation is impossible. First, all sentences *interlock syntactically* as they share the same grammatical constructions. Secondly, theoretical sentences and observational sentences *interlock lexically* in so far observational terms *occur* both in observation sentences and in at least some theoretical sentences. For instance, the observational term 'water' occurs in the observation sentence

(30) Lo! water

and in the theoretical sentence

(31) Water is H_2O.

There is, however, a solution which makes a full-blooded holism consistent with a non adulterated version of empiricism. To secure the compatibility of the two claims, one has simply to say that the observation sentences which should be granted a privileged status by whoever wishes to comply with the requirements of empiricism are *not* the *same* sentences – in a sense of 'same' to be explained shortly – as those which are denied a privileged status by whoever wishes to comply with the requirements of holism.

The solution I propound does not impute to Quine an equivocation over the expression 'observation sentence'. I do not arbitrarily split the set of observation sentences into two jointly exhaustive and mutually exclusive subsets. I simply mean that observation sentences can be *seen* either as *structureless wholes*, (i.e., as one-word sentences), or as *structured wholes*.

When Quine claims that the periphery is made up of sentences directly keyed to experience, what he has in mind are precisely the observation sentences taken as structureless wholes. To support my interpretation, I will simply quote this passage from the *Web of Belief*:

> The special virtue of observation sentences is that we can in principle learn them by ostension as wholes, keyed as wholes to the appropriate observable occasions, before ever learning to link the component words to enduring bodies...
> Learning by ostension, as a trained animal might, to associate whole observation sentences with appropriate patterns of stimulation, is a first indispensable step toward learning physical theory. (Quine and Ullian [1970], p. 25, 26)

If we bear in mind the distinction between observation sentences qua structureless wholes and observation sentences qua structured wholes we can reconcile Quine's two apparently conflicting views:
(a) All sentences are theory-laden to a certain extent (Holism);
(b) Some sentences, namely observation sentences, are the check points for all theories of the world (Empiricism).

If observationality pertains only to sentences taken as *structureless wholes*, it follows that *terms*, as opposed to sentences, are always *theoretical* since they are obtained by analysing sentences i.e. by an operation which necessitates our taking structure into account. Hence to be consistent Quine must drop the distinction between observational terms and theoretical terms. Here again our expectations are fulfilled. Quine holds that the thing-words 'cats, mats, tables' and so on which occur in observation sentences belong to the 'theory' of enduring bodies.

That there are enduring bodies at all, behind the passing show of sensory appearance, is a point of physical theory – a rudimentary point, but still something beyond the observable present occasion. (Quine and Ullian [1970], p. 25)

The point is made again in *Theories and Things* "... I see all objects as theoretical". (Quine [1981a], p. 20)

This is not, however, the only way of escaping Dummett's dilemma. There is another way out. The description of this alternative strategy, however, has to be postponed until we have at our disposal some concepts of Quine's behavioural semantics, such as the concept of 'occasion sentence'.

6. Language and Theory

Quine subscribes to a *verificationist conception* of meaning which he expresses thus:

Say what difference the truth or falsity of a sentence would make to possible experience, and you have said all there is to say about the meaning of the sentence; such, in substantially the words of C.S. Peirce, is the verification theory of meaning. (Quine [1970c], p. 5)

On the other hand, he subscribes to the doctrine we have called '*epistemological holism*' according to which "... our statements about the external world face the tribunal of sense experience not individually but only as a corporate body". (Quine [1951a], p. 41)

What emerges from this if one combines these two theses? Føllesdal replies: "If holism is combined with a Peircean theory of meaning ... it follows that sentences do not generally have meaning one by one." (Føllesdal [1973], p. 290, 291)

Føllesdal's reconstruction of Quine's view can be supported by the following passage:

> The idea of defining a symbol in use was, ..., an advance over the impossible term-by-term empiricism of Locke and Hume. The statement, rather than the term, came with Frege to be recognized as the unit accountable to an empiricist critique. But what I am now urging is that even in taking the statement as unit we have drawn our grid too finely. The unit of empirical significance is the whole of science. (Quine [1951a], p. 42)

Quine's expression 'empirical significance' however is rather obscure. If we equate 'significance' with meaning, it is tempting to describe as *semantic holism* the theory which results from the combination of *epistemological holism* and *Peircean verificationism*. We should, however, refrain from using the expression 'semantic holism' to describe Quine's position in the passage we have just quoted. The contrast between *epistemological holism* and *semantic holism* would make sense for a philosopher who acknowledges a distinction between *theory* and *language*; but it does not make sense for Quine who rejects this familiar distinction just as much as he rejects the analytic-synthetic distinction. He rejects it in favour of a view in which language and theory belong to a *conglomerate*. For this conglomerate, Føllesdal has coined the term 'language-theory'. But how are we to interpret this term?

If one takes the words 'language' and 'theory' in a technical sense, a language is a set L of well formed expressions, and a theory is the set T of theorems of L. If T is consistent, it will always be only a proper subset of L. Thus, if T contains the formula P as a theorem, it cannot contain the negation of P, i.e. $\overline{P}$. So that the only theories that are co-extensive with their languages are inconsistent ones. Hence, on this interpretation of 'language-theory' the term designates only inconsistent theories; which amounts to a *reductio ad absurdum*. There is, however, another interpretation in which Føllesdal's neologism makes sense.

The source of the difficulty arises from the fact that we have tried to understand 'language-theory' from within a *static* and *synchronic* perspective. The remedy is to adopt a different perspective, i.e., one that is *genetic* and *diachronic*. From this perspective it is possible to see how language and theory can be so closely interconnected as to be inseparable from one another.

The first step in the argument is to notice that the point of departure for the language learner is inextricable from the point of departure for the learning of theory. As Quine comments "... observation sentences are the starting-points in the learning of language. Also, they are the starting-points and the check points of scientific theory" (Quine [1975a], p. 73). Quine's point is important, and rests on the fact that when one learns the *meaning* of a word ostensively, one at the same time learns the *truth* of a proposition. It is precisely this *coincidence* of the two kinds of learning that gives force to the 'paradigm case' argument used by philosophers of ordinary language.

Moreover, the overlap between language and theory is not restricted just to the first stages of learning. It is also to be found in the relationship between sensory inputs and theory. Quine has made this point concisely in *The Roots of Reference*: "The evidence relation and the semantical relation of observation to theory are coextensive." (Quine [1974], p. 38)

Language and theory coincide at the *point of departure* (= sensory inputs), and also between the point of departure and the *point of arrival*. Is Quine ready to conclude that they also coincide at the point of arrival? I think that Quine's claim should not be made stronger than it is. Quine is not committed to saying that language and theory are *identical*, he is only committed to saying that language and theory are at most *indiscernable* and at least *inseparable*.

Evidence for this interpretation which is fully consistent with Føllesdal's, can be found in the following passage from *Two Dogmas*

Taken collectively, science has its double dependence upon language and experience; but this duality is not significantly traceable into the statements of science taken one by one. (Quine [1951a], p. 42)

Even this weaker claim concerning the relation between language and theory appeared so paradoxical to Chomsky, that he refused to attribute it to Quine:

... interpretation of Quine's remarks is made difficult at points because of his tendency to use the terms 'language' and 'theory' interchangeably, though obviously he must be presupposing a fundamental difference between the two, he is, for example, surely not proposing that two monolingual speakers of the same language cannot disagree on questions of belief. : . (Chomsky [1968], p. 54)

Chomsky believes, in other words, that it is charitable not to impute to Quine an abandonment of the distinction between verbal disagreements and disagreements in belief. In his eyes, as in those of Grice and Strawson, the distinction is unquestionable. But this very distinction is not unquestionable for Quine, precisely because of his rejection of the distinction between analytic and synthetic statements. As Lauener has aptly remarked, according to Quine

> ... it is not meaningful to maintain in an *absolute* way that a theory is formulable in several languages, or, reciprocally that several theories are expressible in the *same* language. (Lauener [1982], p. 116)

In this context it is worth recalling Quine's comments on the translation of 'q ka bu q' in "Carnap and Logical Truth".

Confirmation of our interpretation, which is suggested by the remarks of Lauener quoted above, is given by Quine's reply to Chomsky. To Chomsky's reproach that he tends to use 'language' and 'theory' interchangeably Quine replies:

> This tendency is related to my rejection of the traditional distinction between analytic and synthetic statements; or, what comes to the same thing, the distinction between meaning and widely shared collateral information; or, what comes in the end to much the same thing again, the notion that the sentences of a theory have their several and separable empirical contents. (Quine [1968b], p. 281)

Later on, when we discuss Quine's semantic theory in detail we shall see that there is yet another reason why Quine should make no sharp separation between language and theory. For him a language is a set of dispositions to accept and reject sentences, and a theory is also a set of dispositions to accept and reject only certain sentences. Though the two sets do not usually coincide they include the same kind of elements.[1]

One final difficulty requires examination. It might seem that if language and theory are inseparable, every change in the latter gives rise to a change in the former, which leads to the paradox of *incommensurability* of scientific theories. Mary Hesse has stated the problem in extremely clear terms:

> We cannot even know that different theories are 'about' the same observational subject matter, for if the meaning of the predicates of observation statements are determined by the theoretical beliefs held by their reporters, and if these meanings differ in different theories, then we seem to have an incommensurability between theories which allows no logical comparison between them, and in particular allows no relations of consistency, incompatibility or relative confirmation. (Hesse [1970], p. 197)

---

[1] I owe this to a referee.

One could avoid the paradox by treating certain observation predicates as invariant; but that would be to revive the analytic-synthetic distinction. But there exists a more subtle solution which enables us to save the distinction between language and theory. This solution again requires us to take up a *diachronic* standpoint. Mary Hesse spells it out in the following passage:

> To save the notion of 'same theory' which is required to avoid the meaning variance paradoxes, there must be some such [semantic] stability, indeed the majority of descriptive predicates must be stable in this sense, but just as we do not know *a priori* which observation statements will be retained as true in the next theory, neither do we know which observation predicates will retain stability of meaning. (Hesse [1970], p. 202)

Hesse's solution takes advantage of the synchronic-diachronic distinction: although changes in theory are most of the time accompanied by changes in language, the two changes do not coincide. Language evolves more slowly. It is more stable than theory.

There is another alternative to Hesse's solution. It is due to Dilworth [1981]. In Dilworth's account allegedly incommensurable theories such as Newton's mechanics, in which mass is independent of velocity, and Einstein's mechanics, in which mass decreases when velocity increases, should not be seen as two sets of sentences which are mutually incompatible in a logical sense, like p and $\sim p$. They should instead be likened to two contrary concepts such as blue and red which cannot be applied to the same spot or to two mutually exclusive interpretations of an ambiguous picture (duck-rabbit).

The best solution might be the second one, i.e. to discard the traditional view of conflicting theories, seen as disjoint subsets of the same language which are related by logical relationships such as mutual contradictoriness, and also to interpret Quine's tendency to blur the distinction between language and theory as a consequence of his blurring the distinction between linguistic change and theory change. The incommensurability problem will be discussed again in connection with Deviant Logics (see Chapter VI, Section 1).

II
The Theory of Meaning

1. Platonism, Mentalism and Behavioural Semantics

The most obvious, indeed commonplace, assertion that the theorist of language can make is undoubtedly the following: sentences are divisible into three subsets: the set of *true* sentences, the set of *false* sentences, and the set of sentences which are *neither true nor false* such as, for instance, sentences containing meaningless expressions.

Another way of saying the same thing, is to say that one can ascribe the predicate 'meaningful' to some sentences and to others the predicate 'meaningless', and that to the former one can then either ascribe the predicate 'true', or the predicate 'false'.

Indeed, to say only this is to say something that is philosophically neutral, and indisputable provided one does not also hold the view that it is propositions rather than sentences that are true or false.

Instead of the predicates 'meaningful', 'true', 'false' some theorists have used much less neutral language to describe the same matters. For example, Frege in 'Sense and Reference', replaces the type-(a) formulations below, with ones of type-(b):

(1) (a) The sentence S is meaningful

     (b) The sentence S has a meaning

(2) (a) The sentence S is true or false

     (b) The sentence S has a truth-value

This replacement is not an insignificant notational variant, but the adoption of a theoretical stance which needs to be grounded by arguments. Grice and Strawson have presented one such argument (Grice and Strawson [1956], p. 85), but it does not hold water; as Quine shows in *Word and Object*:

One of those arguments involves the fallacy of subtraction: it is argued that if we can speak of a sentence as meaningful, or as having meaning, then there must be a meaning that it has, and this meaning will be identical with or distinct from the meaning that another sentence has. This is urged without ... any notice of the fact that we could as well justify the hypostasis of sakes and unicorns on the basis of the idioms 'for the sake of' and 'is hunting unicorns'. (Quine [1960a], p. 206–207)

What Quine rejects in Frege's work is an *avoidable* platonism and, to the extent that it is avoidable, a platonism that is incompatible with the maxim of relative empiricism formulated in the *Roots of Reference* as follows: "Don't venture farther from sensory evidence than you need to." (Quine [1974], p. 138)

The demands that Frege wishes to satisfy are legitimate, but they are not sufficient to justify platonism. Thus, for example, he writes:

A third realm must be recognised. What belongs to this corresponds with ideas, in that it cannot be perceived by the senses, but with things in that it needs no bearer to the contents of whose consciousness to belong. Thus the thought, for example, which we expressed in the Pythagorean theorem is timelessly true, true independently of whether anyone takes it to be true. (Frege [1918–1919], p. 29)

It is clear, however, that the *independence* of truth from the thinking subject can be assured at less cost by, for example, Tarski's semantic theory of truth. One should bear in mind that the *partial* definitions of truth (i.e. valid for one sentence at a time), that are obtained by substituting a sentence for 'p' and the name of this sentence for 'X' in the schema (3):

(3) X is true in L if and only if p

make no allusion at all to an observer; as can be seen, for example, from (4):

(4)   'Snow is white' is true in English if and only if snow is white

In other words, it is necessary and sufficient for the truth of the sentence quoted that snow be white; it is not, therefore, also necessary that there exist men to *see* that it is indeed white, or to *say* that it is.

At this point it might be objected that Tarski's definition is committed to the existence of a language, and that it is impossible to conceive of a language existing independently from its speakers (past, present and future). But this objection also fails. For it is possible to define the notion of a sentence and of a language using only mathematical notions like that of a sequence; sentences, for instance, can be taken as mathematical sequences of their component words or letters.

It might indeed be retorted that this reply commits us to platonism, since it involves the postulation of mathematical objects, such as numbers. But, in the first place, the admission of a realm of numbers, or, at least of sets, is less of a commitment than would be the admission of a universe of Fregean thoughts. We are committed only to extensional, as opposed to intensional,[1] entities. And, in the second place, there exist accounts of numbers and sequences which are compatible with a *non-linguistic* brand of *Nominalism*. (Van Bendegem [1983])

Likewise, it is possible to understand the autonomy of meaning in relation to the speaking subject *without* postulating a third world constituted by *meanings*. It is sufficient to accord to 'meaningful' its initial status as a monadic predicate of *sentences*.

An alternative to Frege's platonic semantics – a mentalistic semantics – is outlined by Russell in *An Inquiry into Meaning and Truth* (1940): "Speaking generally, language of the sort that logicians would call 'assertion' has two functions: to indicate a fact, and to express a state of the speaker" (Russell [1940], p. 212). To this psychological state Russell gives the name 'proposition', and he goes on:

> I conclude ... that it is necessary to distinguish propositions from sentences, but that propositions need not be indefinable. They are to be defined as psychological occurrences of certain sorts – complex images, expectations, etc. Such occurrences are "expressed" by sentences ... When two sentences have the same meaning, that is because they express the same proposition. (Russell [1940], p. 189)

Quine, however, rejects Russell's mentalistic semantics as forcefully as he does Frege's platonistic semantics. He objects that synonymy is too fleeting a notion to bear the weight that Russell wants to put on it:

> Readers have supposed that my complaint [against mentalistic semantics] is ontological; it is not. If in general I could make satisfactory sense of declaring two expressions to be synonymous, I would be more than pleased to recognize an abstract object as their common meaning. The method is familiar: I would define the meaning of an expression as the set of its synonyms. Where the trouble lies, rather, is

---

[1] Initially the *intension* was held to consist of the properties which go to make up a concept whereas the extension was the set of things falling under the concept. Later the dichotomy between intension and extension also came to be applied in connection with linguistic expressions, names, predicates and sentences. The intensional entities associated with these three linguistic categories are respectively individual concept, property or relation-in-intension, and proposition. (See Haller [1982], Gochet [1980])

in the two-place predicate of synonymy itself; it is too desperately wanting in clarity and perspicuity. (Quine [1977a], pp. 166–167)

Russell and the British Empiricists are the target of this passage in the *Roots of Reference:*

Language, we are told, serves to convey ideas. When we learn language we learn to associate its words with the same ideas with which other speakers associate them. Now how do we know that these ideas are the same? And, so far as communication is concerned, who cares? We have all learned to apply the word 'red' to blood, tomatoes, ripe apples and boiled lobsters. The associated idea, the associated sensation, is as may be. Language bypasses the idea and homes on the object. Than the idea there is little less useful to the study of language. (Quine [1974], p. 35)

If one rejects "the myth of a museum in which the exhibits are meanings and the words are labels" (Quine [1969], p. 27), one ought to look for an *alternative* to platonistic semantics as much as to mentalistic semantics. This alternative Quine seeks in a semantics inspired by the naturalism defended by Dewey during the last three decades of his life, a naturalism that is expressed in the following passages cited by Quine himself in *Ontological Relativity and Other Essays*: "Meaning ... is not a psychic existence; it is primarily a property of behavior" (Dewey [1925] quoted in Quine [1969], p. 27). And later: "language is specifically a mode of interaction of at least two beings, a speaker and a hearer; it presupposes an organized group to which these creatures belong, and from whom they have acquired their habits of speech. It is therefore a relationship." (Dewey [1925], quoted in Quine, [ibid.], p. 125)

Quine's most detailed exposition of his naturalistic theory of meaning is to be found in the lengthy second chapter of *Word and Object*. We shall now examine his extremely original theory.

2. Radical Translation and Behaviourism

When one speaks of synonymy one usually has in mind the synonymy of words or sentences of the same language. The study of *intralinguistic synonymy* is not, however, the ideal field for the full deployment of a semantic methodology. In effect, when studying his native tongue the linguist is in a privileged situation. To discover the sense of a word it is sufficient for him to consult his 'linguistic competence', or to consult his fellow native speakers. By contrast, a linguist who faces the task of translating a culturally isolated language for the first time, that is, a linguist who is employed in constructing a grammar and a bilingual dictionary enabling one to match *interlinguistically synonymous sentences*, is constrained by the nature of things to accommodate himself to a purely naturalistic and behaviourist approach to linguistic phenomena. No other approach is possible: the jungle linguist is condemned to behaviourism.

The jungle linguist has certain sensory stimulations σ in the circumstances C. He observes that the native is placed in the same circumstances, that is, that he observes the same thing from (roughly) the same angle. He then infers that the native has very similar stimulations to himself on the rather uncontroversial assumption that he has the same perceptual apparatus.[1]

Having made these observations, assumptions, and inferences, the linguist can now begin work. At this stage he can study the use of language as he would study any other natural phenomena. He is limited to *observing* correlations between (a) the sensory stimulations which he assumes that both he and the native share, (b) the verbal behaviour of the native, and to making inductions on the basis of these observations. In fact, matters are not as simple as this, since a third factor has to be taken into account, namely, the *non-verbal* behaviour of the native, the study of which may require a hermeneutic approach which is suspect to Quine. But to simplify, we shall ignore this third factor.

3. Stimulus Meaning

A theory of meaning aiming to be empirical ought to include in its foundations a concept of meaning defined in terms of sensory stimulations and verbal reactions. Therefore, Quine introduces the concept of *stimulus meaning* at the outset of his theory.

The stimulus meaning of the sentence S for a speaker a at time t is the ordered pair of sets $\langle \Sigma, \Sigma' \rangle$ in which Σ is the set of the stimulations which would cause a to assent to S at t and Σ' is the set of the stimulations which would cause a to dissent from S at t. Such is the definition of the stimulus

---

[1] I owe this to Susan Haack.

meaning centered on stimulation. Considered from the point of view of the audience which hears the sentence and has to interpret it, the stimulus meaning of the sentence S for a speaker a is the battery of a's dispositions either to assent to or dissent from S when affected by the stimulations σ and σ'.

However, the notion of stimulus meaning is soon seen not to include all that is normally meant by 'meaning'. *This is not, however, a reason for rejecting the concept as inadequate*, for to do so would, at the same time, be to renounce the ambition of laying the foundations of an empirical semantics. Rather than reject the concept as too simple minded, let us, in the following sections, examine closely the gap that exists between the concept of *stimulus meaning* and that of meaning itself. But one objection must be disposed of straight away.

Not so long ago Condillac was criticized for the *abstract* and *speculative* character of his fundamental notion, that of sensation. But isn't Quine's notion of sensory stimulation exposed to the same reproach? Are there identity conditions for stimulations? If not, statements of the form 'σ_1 is the *same stimulation* as σ_2', would be no better placed than ones of the form 'S_1 has the *same meaning* as S_2'.

Without going into too much detail, it can be said straight away that Quine has foreseen this objection and guarded himself against it. What might be accomplished by talking of sameness of stimulations is accomplished by talking of *receptual*, as opposed to perceptual, *similarity*.

Receptual similarity is a relation between physical events, that is between the states of the nerve endings of a living subject which receives stimulations. It can be defined as follows:

The receptual similarity of a subject's episodes is the mere physical similarity of impact on the subject's sensory surface, regardless of behavior. (Gibson, [1982], p. 7–8)

Unlike the notion of perception that of reception defined in *The Roots of Reference* is fully in accordance with the standards of behaviourism.

4. Occasion, Standing, Eternal, Observational and Theoretical Sentences

Quine introduced a distinction which plays a central role in his semantics, namely the distinction between *occasion* and *standing* sentences. *Occasion sentences* only prompt the assent or dissent of the native speaker if the ethnologist asks a question immediately after an appropriate stimulation (for example 'It-hurts', 'This-is-red', and 'Here-is-a-rabbit' which we have spelled with hyphens to emphasize that they are associated with stimulations as wholes just as would be the one word sentence '*Piove*', i.e. 'it is raining'). On the contrary, *standing sentences* are sentences to which the speaker can reiterate his assent, or from which he can reiterate his dissent without being prompted to do so by a concomitant stimulation (for example, 'President *A* is dead', '*The Times* has come').

Eternal sentences are a subclass of the standing sentences, they are "sentences that stay forever true, or forever false, independently of any special circumstances under which they happen to be uttered or written" (Quine [1960a], p. 36). Amongst them the sentences of arithmetic naturally occur, since features of times and place are not relevant to a science like arithmetic. The same can be said of the laws of physics; but the class of eternal sentences also includes such sentences as "It *rains* in Boston on the 14th July 1968" in which the verb is treated as tenseless.

Quine had forerunners. When he describes the above mentioned sentence as an eternal sentence as soon as the event described has occurred, he operates with the concept of *necesse per accidens* which the twelfth century Scholastics borrowed from Aristotle.

Just as it is desirable to distinguish the subclass of eternal sentences within the class of standing sentences, there is also good reason for distinguishing within the class of occasion sentences (for example, 'Here is a rabbit', 'Here is a spy'), the subclass of *observation sentences*. As we saw, these are not limited to the description of dubious private entities such as *sense-data* (for example, 'A red spot appears at this moment'), they can also refer to *physical objects* which enjoy the status of public entities (for example, 'Here is a rabbit'). Quine's classification can, therefore, be summarized as follows:

	Standing sentences		Occasion sentences
eternal	$3+3=6$ The postman passes (tenseless) by on the 9–8–1980, at 9 a.m. G.M.T.	*observational*	Dog (Here-is-a-dog) Rabbit (Here-is-a-rabbit)
non eternal	The crocuses have come out The postman has passed by	*non observational*	Spy (Here-is-a-spy) Bachelor (Here-is-a-bachelor)

Note, finally, that exactly what falls into one category rather than another depends on what we count as the maximum duration of a stimulation. It is not necessary to conclude, however, that Quine defends a 'gradualism' in which all his distinctions ultimately become blurred. The contrast between the most pure *observation sentences* and the *standing sentences* remains unaffected: the former, *taken as wholes*, have a sense *individually*, whereas the latter are *interdependent*. In other words, Quine attributes an *autonomous* empirical content to occasion-observation sentences, and does so to them *alone*.

5. The Relation Between Observation Sentences and Holism Revisited

As we have seen, only occasion-observation sentences have an autonomous meaning, in the sense that they can be understood as a *structureless whole* by association with publicly observable stimulations. Which is not to say that they ordinarily *should* be understood in this way. By contrast a theory contains nothing but *standing sentences*. To be assimilated into the theory, occasion-observation sentences first have to be transformed into standing sentences. This calls for the elimination of indexical items and of grammatical indications of tense. Thus, the occasion sentence 'Lo, a flash of light' will be replaced by 'There *is* a flash of light at place p at time t' (with tenseless 'is'). In other words, a theory does not contain occasion-observation sentences, but records of them, which are standing sentences, and indeed eternal sentences.

It is therefore possible for Quine to maintain consistently both of the following theses:

(a) Occasion-observation sentences are *learned* and verified *individually*, and

(b) No sentence belonging to a theory, even an observation sentence has its own *autonomous* content. Holism can, therefore, be maintained *without restriction*. This is the second reply which can be made to Dummett's objection (see p. 31).

One should note an interesting feature of Quine's notion of observation sentence. When this notion is given a behavioural definition, as it is by Quine, for whom an observation sentence is one which, given an appropriate situation, commands general assent, it becomes a much clearer notion than the classical one defined in terms of sense data. As Quine observes

The *behavioural* notion of an observation sentence is a distinct one – not a fuzzy one – which admits of degrees: The degree of observationality of a sentence might ... be measured inversely by the average dose of stimulation needed to induce a stable verdict. (Quine [1970a], p. 5)

6. The Distinction Between Meaning and Collateral Information for Observation Sentences

We saw that only occasion sentences prompt the informant's assent (or dissent) *solely* when the ethnologist pronounces them immediately after the appropriate intersubjective stimulation. And of these only observation sentences are regularly correlated with sets of stimulations. In the case of the sentence 'Rabbit' the stimulations that are part of its affirmative stimulus-meaning have a *salient-distinctive trait*; they present to the ethnologist, as to the natives themselves, a common *anatomical configuration* which enables him to generalise by *induction* on the basis of several examples. No such thing is the case with 'Here is a spy' or 'Here is a bachelor' – which are occasion sentences that are not observation sentences – and there can be no question of noting a common observable trait in this case, as Quine notes:

Now a similar effort with a non-observational native occasion sentence, of the type of our 'Bachelor', would have bogged down in its early stages. Sample stimulations belonging to the affirmative stimulus meaning of such a sentence, for the given native, would show no tempting common traits by which to conjecture further cases, or none but such as fail to hold up on further tries. (Quine [1960a], p. 46)

It would seem, therefore, that it is only in the case of observation sentences that the technical concept of *stimulus meaning* has any chance of being a good *explicans* of the notion of *meaning* in current usage, and, only there, likewise, that the concept of *stimulus synonymy* has one of being a good *explicans* of the notion of *synonymy*. But even if one limits oneself to these special cases, the technical concept proposed does not seem to be adequate.

On reflection unforeseen problems loom into view:

... sameness of stimulus meaning has its shortcomings as a synonymy relation. The difficulty is that an informant's assent to or dissent from 'Gavagai?' can depend excessively on prior collateral information as a supplement to the present prompting stimulus. He may assent on the occasion of nothing better than an ill-glimpsed movement in the grass, because of his earlier observation, unknown to the linguist, of rabbits near the spot. (Quine [1960a], p. 37)

In the situation just evoked the ethnologist is able to eliminate the parasitic intervention of collateral information by varying his informants, but there are cases in which this method is inoperative because the whole native community possesses the information. Davidson imagines a case in which the sight of a certain fly, a local 'rabbit fly', unknown to the linguist and recognizable from afar by its long wings and erratic movements, might help the natives to recognize as a rabbit an animal that was barely glimpsed. In this case Quine remarks that

Ocular irradiations combining poor glimpses of rabbits with good ones of rabbit-flies would belong to the stimulus meaning of 'Gavagai' for natives generally, and not to that of 'Rabbit' for the linguist. (Quine [1960a], p. 37)

This time the most subtle experimental techniques will not succeed in disassociating the sense of 'Gavagai' from collateral information. Should one conclude, therefore, that the concept of stimulus meaning is bankrupt? Such a pessimistic conclusion would be unjustified. All that this example shows is that the distinction between meaning and collateral information possessed in common by the members of a linguistic community has no *experimental sense*. One cannot say at what point an *increase in information* finishes and a *change of meaning* begins. As Quine says:

What we objectively have is just an evolving adjustment to nature, reflected in an evolving set of dispositions to be prompted by stimulations to assent to or dissent from sentences. (Quine [1960a], pp. 38–39)

7. The Meaning of Non-Observational Occasion Sentences

We saw in the previous section that non-observational occasion sentences cannot be regularly correlated with an observable trait, and that this would seem to be a further obstacle to the identification of stimulus meaning with meaning itself. But is it?

The sense of a sentence of the type 'Here is a bachelor' is inculcated

... through connections with other sentences, linking up thus indirectly with past stimulations of other sorts than those that serve directly to prompt present assent to the sentence ... (Quine [1960a], p. 45)

The stimulus meaning of such a sentence will, therefore, vary with the speaker's past, even though the network of sentence to sentence connections be much the same for each speaker.

It seems, therefore, that stimulus meaning differs greatly from meaning itself in the case of non-observational occasion sentences, and it is tempting, therefore, to refuse to give the concept an explanatory role. But Quine noticed a surprising fact which proves the worth of his concept of stimulus meaning:

But curiously enough the stimulus meanings of 'Bachelor' and 'Unmarried man' are, despite all this, identical for any one speaker. An individual would at any one time be prompted by the same stimulations to assent to 'Bachelor' and 'Unmarried man'; and similarly for dissent. *Stimulus synonymy*, or sameness of stimulus meaning, is as good a standard of synonymy for non-observational occasion sentences as for observation sentences as long as we stick to one speaker. (Quine [1960a], p. 46)

One can, moreover, lift the restriction to a single speaker and say that 'Bachelor' and 'Unmarried man' are stimulus synonymous for the *whole community* of the English speaking subjects in the sense that they are so for each of its members. Finally, 'Bachelor' and 'Soltero' can be said to be *stimulus synonymous* for the English-Spanish bilingual. Thus, contrary to all expectation, the relations between *stimulus synonymy* and *synonymy* in the case of non-observational occasion sentences are not a trivial reduplication of those between stimulus meaning and meaning. When one takes speakers *one by one* stimulus synonymy seems to be a good *explicans* of synonymy itself in occasion sentences: the gap that existed between stimulus meaning and meaning has disappeared. The concepts of behaviourist semantics thus open up a new field of inquiry. But we should withdraw the word 'explicans' in this context. Quine does not try to work out a behaviouristic *reconstruction* of the concepts of synonymy or analyticity, as Carnap does. (Ricketts [1982], p. 132)

8. The Limits of Naturalism and of the Experimental Method

We saw that the ethnologist begins by determining the sense of observation sentences, starting with the *passive observation* of a constant correlation between the same stimulations of the native's senses and the same linguistic reactions on his part. This is simply a *commonplace use of induction* which is in no way different from the use of induction applied to natural phenomena by which men have learned, for instance, that thunder follows lightning.

But the ethnologist cannot stop at this point. Observation is insufficient to discover that the class of stimulations capable of triggering the one word sentence 'Gavagai', that is to say 'Rabbit', is *contained* in and not excluded by the class capable of triggering the one word sentence 'Animal'. Indeed, in virtue of the physical law that one can only pronounce one sentence at a time, the 'passive' ethnologist who understands the native to say 'Here is a rabbit' has no way of knowing whether the same native could have said 'Here is an animal' as well. Like all *physical events*, sensory stimulations can enter into a physical relation of *temporal succession* and *contiguity*, but they cannot enter into a logical relationship such as *membership* or *inclusion*. Passive observation of the sensory stimulations which trigger the utterances of 'Rabbit' and 'Animal' does not, therefore, enable one to discover that each time the native says the former he could have said the latter. In this case a more subtle method will be necessary: the ethnologist will have to exchange a merely passive role for an active one, and to utter sentences himself in the native's presence when the appropriate sensory stimulation is produced. In order to interpret the native's response, he will need, however, to have previously identified the signs of assent and dissent in the native's language, that is to have understood the native's words for 'yes' and 'no'.

These moves go beyond *observation* and *induction* however, since the *experimental method* and the *hypothetico-deductive method* are brought into play by them, though it is still the case that only methods currently used in the natural sciences are made use of. This is no longer the case, however, when the linguist comes to grip with *standing sentences* or with occasion sentences seen as *structured wholes*, i.e. as compounds of words syntactically related (which is the standard account).

9. Analytical Hypotheses

To understand (a) *non-observational occasion sentences*, for example, 'Lo, a bachelor', (b) *standing sentences*, for example 'Lions eat gazelles', and even to understand observational occasion sentences as compounds *analysable* into components, the linguist must understand (a) the sense of individual words, and (b) the semantic role of the syntactical constructions the sentences contain. For example, he must understand the effect that the position of a word in relation to another has on the overall sense of the containing expression; 'Lions eat gazelles' does not have the same sense as, the more startling 'Gazelles eat lions', even though each sentence contains the same words.

How then is the linguist to proceed at this point? In Quine's view he must have recourse to a new technique which he calls the method of 'analytical hypotheses'.

He [The linguist] segments heard utterances into conveniently short recurrent parts, and thus compiles a list of native "words". Various of these he hypothetically equates to English words and phrases, in such a way as to conform to (1)–(4) [constraints imposed by stimulus meaning]. (Quine [1960a], p. 68)

It is important to note, at this point, that *every* segmentation of a sentence into words requires the use of analytical hypotheses, even if the sentence belongs to the most elementary category. Thus, for instance, if we wish to understand an occasion-observation sentence such as 'Lo, a rabbit!' *analytically*, rather than *as-a-whole*, we must have recourse to analytical hypotheses. The privileged status of occasion-observation sentences does not extend to their lexical constituents. It should also be added that the linguist ought to compile a list of *morphemes*, as well as a list of *lexemes*, to account for such differences as that between 'Piove' ('It is raining) and 'Piovera' ('It will rain'). An even more subtle treatment is needed to account for the one word Latin sentence 'i' ('go!'). But these are refinements, which do not substantially affect Quine's thesis.

Analyses made by the linguist of a sentence into words are *conjectural*; hence, Quine calls them 'analytical hypotheses'. One might think, therefore, that analytical hypotheses are comparable to the hypotheses of other sciences which use the *hypothetico-deductive* method. Quine, however, has developed an extremely controversial thesis, the Indeterminacy of Translation, which commits him to denying just this.

10. The Indeterminacy of Translation

Quine's controversial thesis depends on two key points.

a) It is possible to construct *rival* analytical hypotheses each of which is compatible with the native's disposition to speech behaviour, but which nevertheless attribute different *meanings* (intensions) to standing sentences, and even different *references* (extensions) to some of their constituents.

b) Moreover, not only is it not possible to know which is the better hypothesis, but there does not exist a translation of the disputed cases, which is *objectively* preferable. In other words, there is no objective reason for saying that one set of analytical hypotheses is correct rather than another. Thus, the translator is not in the position of the sculptor, evoked by Quine, who was trying to restore a sculpture of Hercules of which only the foot remained. In that case there is a reality, the missing torso, which the sculptor tries to reproduce faithfully. In the case of translation, however, there is no objective reality analogous to the torso. Semantics therefore suffers, in Quine's view, from a deficiency which other sciences happily do not suffer from. Analytical hypotheses are more like conventions than like scientific hypotheses.

The claim (b) has been formulated in an extremely clear way in *Facts of the Matter*:

... two translators might develop independent manuals of translation, both of them compatible with all speech behavior and all dispositions to speech behavior, and yet one manual would offer translations that the other translator would reject. My position was that either manual could be useful, but as to which was right and which wrong there was no fact of the matter. (Quine [1977a], p. 167)

The indeterminacy of translation is therefore not just *epistemological*, but *ontological*.

This thesis has been widely discussed. Friedman rightly says that

Quine's thesis of the indeterminacy of translation is probably the most well known and widely discussed thesis in contemporary philosophy. (Friedman [1975], p. 353)

We will also add that it is extremely debatable.

However, before looking at it critically, we shall first carefully examine Quine's own arguments for it. Quine begins by establishing the following premiss: rival semantic interpretations, obtained by analysing the same native sentence by use of analytical hypotheses, do not lend themselves to a crucial test which would choose at most one of them, disqualifying the others. Indeed, the test itself depends on the adoption of certain analytical hypotheses. It is, therefore, always possible to 'save' a translation manual by changing some of the other analytical hypotheses involved in the allegedly crucial test.

A famous example of Quine's helps to make this clearer. He considers a situation in which "... a certain heathen expression is one to which natives can be prompted to assent by the presence of a rabbit, or reasonable *facsimile*, and not otherwise". (Quine [1969], p. 2)

In this situation Quine writes "an actual field linguist would be sensible enough to equate 'gavagai' with 'rabbit', automatically dismissing such perverse alternatives as 'undetached rabbit part' and 'rabbit stage'" (Quine [1969], p. 34). If he does, however, he jumps to a conclusion which goes far beyond empirical evidence. As Quine puts it in *Word and Object:*

When from the sameness of stimulus meanings of 'Gavagai' and 'Rabbit' the linguist leaps to the conclusion that a gavagai is a whole enduring rabbit, he is just taking for granted that the native is enough like us to have a brief general term for rabbits and no brief general term for rabbit stages or parts. (Quine [1960a], p. 52)

What Quine objects to however is not the recourse to conjectures and hypotheses which is quite common practice in the natural sciences, in which no indeterminacy is to be deplored. What he does question is the peculiar nature of these conjectures and hypotheses. In the following passage, Quine makes this point most vividly:

The method of analytical hypotheses is a way of catapulting oneself into the jungle language by the momentum of the home language. It is a way of grafting exotic shoots on to the old familiar bush ... (Quine [1960a], p. 70)

In other words, the linguist engaged in radical translation behaves almost like a student of animal psychology who interprets animal behaviour on the basis of *anthropomorphic* hypotheses. Is there any way out of this *ethnocentric predicament* which bedevils the jungle linguist?

At this point, it is tempting to argue that the puzzle could be solved by the linguist if he could identify the native equivalents of the definite article, plural morpheme, etc. that is, the interrelated grammatical constructions which enable an English speaker to master the mechanisms of individuation. Once this preliminary task has been performed, the linguist can go a step further and pose the question: 'Is this rabbit the same as that one?' or, rather, the equivalent of this question in the native's language.

Unfortunately, this solution fails. For in order to master the grammatical constructions which are involved in the allegedly crucial question, the linguist has to resort to other analytical hypotheses. The problem is, therefore, not resolved, only displaced. For we still remain enclosed in the circle of analytical hypotheses.

Now, and this is the crucial point, it is possible to have rival sets of analytical hypotheses which pass *ex aequo* all behavioural tests involving dispositions to assent, etc:

There seem bound to be systematically very different choices, all of which do justice to all dispositions to verbal behavior on the part of all concerned. (Quine [1969], p. 34)

The facts about stimulus meaning do not enable us to say that 'gavagai' is synonymous with 'rabbit', nor even that it is simply 'coextensive'. They do not even enable us to say that it is a *count-noun*, as is the English word 'rabbit', rather than a *mass-term*[1]. But, as we have seen, recourse to analytical hypotheses does not fare better. Suppose that the linguist wants to know whether the native who uses the word 'gavagai' refers to an individual or to a collection of undetached parts. To remove all misunderstanding he will try to ask the question 'Is this gavagai the same as that?'. Unfortunately, compensatory adjustments in the translations of other parts of the sentence may both *perpetuate* and *mask* the misunderstanding:

For if one workable overall system of analytical hypotheses provides for translating a given native expression into "is the same as", perhaps another equally workable but systematically different system would translate that native expression rather into something like "belongs with". (Quine [1969], p. 33)

---

[1] To know what a *mass term* "X" refers to requires that we know how much of what goes on counts as *x* and how much does not. One knows what water refers to if one can differentiate it from what is no water. To know what *a count* term "x" refers to, one also has to know how much of what goes on counts as *an x*. For instance, to know what "rabbit" refers to, one must not only be able to differentiate rabbits from dogs but one must also be able to distinguish between two occurrences of the same rabbit and one occurrence of two rabbits.

11. A Critique of the Thesis that Translation is Indeterminate

Of the two points (a) and (b) mentioned at the beginning of the previous section Quine so far has established only the first. He has proved, that is, that there is an epistemological under-determination of translation manuals with respect to behavioural data, but he has in no way established point (b), i.e., shown that there is an *ontological indeterminacy* which is both different from and additional to epistemological under-determination. And it is (b) that is needed to distinguish analytical hypotheses from ordinary scientific ones, and to show that the indeterminacy of translation, with respect to behavioural data of the appropriate kind, differs from the under-determination of physical theories with respect to observations.

Quine has tried to defend (b) as follows:

... theory in physics is an ultimate parameter. There is no legitimate first philosophy, higher or firmer than physics, to which to appeal over physicists' heads.
... Though linguistics is of course a part of the theory of nature, the indeterminacy of translation is not just inherited as a special case of the underdetermination of our theory of nature. It is parallel but additional ...
Consider... the totality of truths of nature, known and unknown, observable and unobservable, past and future. The point about indeterminacy of translation is that it withstands even all this truth, the whole truth about nature. This is what I mean by saying that, where indeterminacy of translation applies, there is no real question of right choice; there is no fact of the matter even to *within* the acknowledged under-determination of a theory of nature. (Quine, [1968b], p. 275.)

Imagine, for example that two physical theories B and B' are different but each compatible with all possible observations. B is an infinite set of sentences $S_1, S_2, S_3 \ldots$, whilst B' is an infinite set of sentences $S'_1, S'_2, S'_3 \ldots$. Given that B and B' are underdetermined, there could be no reason to choose between these two manuals of translation:

$$B \begin{Bmatrix} S_1 \to S'_1 \\ S_2 \to S'_2 \\ S_3 \to S'_3 \end{Bmatrix} B' \qquad B \begin{Bmatrix} S_1 \to S'_1 \\ S_2 S'_2 \\ S_3 S'_3 \end{Bmatrix} B'$$

The tempting reply at this point is that there is a relevant criterion involved in the choice of a translation manual, namely, *simplicity*: just as in physics one would choose Copernicus' heliocentrism rather than Ptolemy's geocentrism – all other things being equal – because of its much greater simplicity. So one would choose the simplest correlation between $S_1 \ldots S_n$ and $S'_1 \ldots S'_n$ as the best translation. Why then cannot the criterion of simplicity be used to establish a *partial ordering* between translation manuals? Quine's reply is that the relation 'more simple translation than' is not an ordering relation:

the most simple mapping of a language A onto one B, followed by the simplest of B onto C, does not necessarily yield the simplest of A onto C. And the simplest mapping of A onto B, followed by the simplest of B onto A, does not necessarily map each element of A onto itself. (Quine, quoted in Føllesdal [1973], p. 295)

Let me offer an example to make this rather concise statement clearer. Consider the translation of "John met his uncle" into Latin, a language in which there is a different word for maternal and paternal uncle. If we translate back from Latin into English we shall be forced to write "John met his paternal uncle" or "John met his maternal uncle" depending on which Latin word was used. Here we have a case where the Latin sentence S_2 is a translation of the English sentence S_1 whereas the English sentence S_1 is not a translation of the Latin sentence S_2. (I owe this point to Prof. Hubien.)

One can also question the simplicity criterion on other grounds. Take, for instance, the case of a foreigner whose thoughts are too complex to be expressed in simple terms in the home language. In this case the translator would clearly be ill advised to choose what would be the simplest mapping of L onto L' seen from the translator's point of view.[1]

The failure of the simplicity criterion, however, does not suffice to establish that the choice between rival manuals of translation is more arbitrary than the choice between rival scientific hypotheses. Manuals of translation might have constraints of their own to comply with.

To establish this point let us shift to a related topic, the theory of acquisition of the mother tongue. The child is in a position comparable to that of the jungle linguist: he cannot decipher standing sentences unless he first dismembers occasion observational sentences into words and extracts grammatical constructions from them, but this task requires making use of *analytical hypotheses*.

The interest of this shift of perspective lies in the constraints which it imports into semantics. As Moravcsik observes:

---

[1] I owe this point to Tyler Burge.

Some semantic theories have developed without regard to questions of learnability ... [A] theory of language, however, must be under the constraint that it cannot postulate semantic structures that would be impossible to learn by a human within the normal contexts. (Moravcsik [1975], p. 56)

Considerations of learnability can be brought to bear on the choice of rival manuals of translation. Take, for instance, a language in which every general term "determines ... the class of those physical objects of which the term can be truly predicated" (Quine [1981a], p. 16). Let us now consider two manuals of translation A and B. The A-manual just maps the terms of the language onto themselves. The B-manual reconstrues "every class systematically as its complement and then compensates for the switch by reinterpreting the dyadic general term 'member of' to mean what had been meant by 'not a member of'" (ibid).

These two manuals are not equally good. Moravcsik's learnability constraint clearly disqualifies the second manual. Predicates such as 'not pencil', 'not pen' are not learnable unless construed as parasitic on predicates such as 'pencil' or 'pen'.

So far we have tried to do no more than establish that the Indeterminacy Thesis is *unsupported* at a crucial point. However, we shall consider whether it is not more deeply compromised. We shall concentrate on a derivative form of indeterminacy, that is the inscrutability of reference.

12. Inscrutability of Reference

In *Word and Object*, Quine analyses the linguistic operation of pointing at some object and in this context he introduces the notion of 'inscrutability of reference'. To set the stage let us imagine that a rabbit scurries past and that the native points to it. The following problem arises.

Two pointings may be pointings to a numerically identical rabbit, to numerically distinct rabbit parts, and to numerically distinct rabbit stages; the inscrutability lies not in resemblance, but in the anatomy of sentences. We could equate a native expression with any of the disparate English terms 'rabbit', 'rabbit stage', 'undetached rabbit part', etc., and still, by compensatorily juggling the translation of numerical identity and associated particles, preserve conformity to stimulus meanings of occasion sentences. (Quine [1960a], p. 53–54)

This puzzle reminds us of the question "Is 'gavagai' synonymous with or coextensive with 'rabbit' or with 'rabbit stage'?" Yet there is a difference. What is at stake now is *reference* as opposed to *meaning*. However one might wonder whether the *compensatory juggling* that is possible is as *free* and *unconstrained* as Quine takes it to be. This question calls for a qualified answer.

Ladmiral who is both a translator and a translation theorist acknowledges the need of compensatory adjustments, but he does not ascribe them the same role as Quine. To appreciate the difference the reader should know that Ladmiral locates translation at the level of *speech* rather than that of *language*. In *Traduire: théorèmes pour la traduction*, he writes:

Speech is the genuine message of the speaker, and of the author, who puts language to work. At the end of this interaction there is a text – which is entirely information.

For each minimal *bit* of information at any linguistic level whatever in the source-text, the problem is therefore to know whether ... the aforementioned information belongs to the speech of the author, or only to the source-language which he uses. In the first case it is necessary to 'convey the information'; in the second case one will content oneself with putting the resources offered by the target language to work, to the highest standards of composition which the construction of a good target text obeys. (Ladmiral [1979], pp. 223–24)

According to Ladmiral, translators are entitled to make use of what he himself, independently of Quine, calls 'compensations' and these adjustments are done individually 'au coup par coup'. (Ladmiral [1979], p. 254)

Ladmiral's argument does not support Quine's thesis in the least since it *presupposes* that the translator has become a bilingual who is capable of making a distinction between what belongs to the information conveyed by the text from what belongs to the source-language. However, as we have seen Quine disputes the bilingual's credentials. On Quine's view, the bilingual is not better off than his fellow man. Quine is considering bridging the gap between languages:

My point remains; for my point is then that another bilingual could have a semantic correlation incompatible with the first bilingual's without deviating from the first bilingual in his speech dispositions within either language, except in his dispositions to translate. (Quine [1960a], p. 74)

Yet there is more to say about bilinguals than Quine allows. Plainly a bilingual must be able to map the virtually *infinite* set of the source language onto the virtually *infinite* set of the target language. If there are manuals of translation at all, i.e. if there are *finite* accounts of this potentially *infinite* capacity, the 'compensatory juggling' above cannot be completely *ad hoc*.

This point has been made forcefully by Holdcroft. The latter invites us to consider a language which "looks just like English, and whose only difference from English is that it contains the word 'gavagai', but not 'rabbit'" (Holdcroft [forthcoming]). Suppose the linguist has to translate

(5)   This is the same gavagai as the one you shot at yesterday.

He could translate (5) as either (5a) or (5b)

(5a)   This is the same rabbit as the one you shot at yesterday

(5b)   This is not the same rabbit stage as the one you shot at yesterday.

but, continues Holdcroft, hearing

(6)   Jim and Bill shot at the same gavagai

uttered in circumstances in which they both shot at the same time at the same rabbit, the linguist would hardly welcome both (6a) and (6b) as alternatives:

(6a)   Jim and Bill shot at the same rabbit

(6b)   Jim and Bill shot at a different rabbit stage.

Of course, "he could translate the native 'same' by the English word 'same' in (6b) as well as (6a), conjecturing that sometimes it means what we mean by 'same', and sometimes what we mean by 'different'". (Holdcroft [forthcoming])

Clearly if completely *ad hoc* juggling is tolerated, i.e., if meaning depends on the *context* alone and is never constrained by *surface syntax*, then Moravcsik's problem arises in an acute form: how can such a language be *learnt* at all?

Quine, however, has described a case of inscrutability which cannot be blamed on an over tolerant conception of compensatory juggling. Rooted as it is in a *grammatical construction* it affects all *translations* systematically. Let us describe it succinctly. In Japanese there exist particles, called 'classifiers', which can be analysed in two ways. According to the first analysis, classifiers attach to numerical adjectives to form composite numerals appropriate for counting distinct types of objects. According to the second, classifiers are not part of a numerical adjective, but rather of a substantive term.

Suppose that the substantive is 'ox' ('cow' or 'horse' etc), the numerical adjective 'five', and that the classifier is what would be expressed in English by 'animal'. Whichever analysis is adopted the *three* Japanese words are translated into English by a pair of words, but the pair has a different sense in the two cases. To bring out the semantic difference, the two interpretations can be rendered by the following English expressions: 'five-animal oxen' (in which 'five-animal' is a numeral whose use is restricted to animals), and 'five head of cattle'. (Quine [1969], p. 36)

Quine's example is hardly conclusive, it might well be argued that "the difference between the two examples is not important since 'five cows' and 'five head of cattle' both present us with five *animals*" (Glotzbach [1979], p. 315). This is the view which Glotzbach defends. A further example discussed by Glotzbach is worth examining in depth, since it shows why the difference stressed by Quine may not be all that significant.

Glotzbach considers the following sentences:

(7) You can't step into the same *river* twice,

(8) You can't step into the same *river-stage* twice,

(9) You can't step into the same *collection* of *river-stages* twice.

Of these, (8) is true, whilst (7) and (9) are false. Suppose that a speaker treats pairs of sentences that differ only as do (7) and (9) as truth-functionally equivalent. In that case, Glotzbach argues

... it would become unreasonable (from the standpoint of the principles governing inductive justification) to continue the search for contexts in which rivers and collections of river-stages differ for her. It seems to me that none of this is in any way exceptional, yet on Quine's views it should be fraught with referential indeterminacy (at least "in principle"). (Glotzbach [1979], p. 291)

This argument is convincing. Admittedly, 'river' and 'collection of river-stages' cease to be co-referential, i.e., to refer to the same object, if the ontological commitments (see Chapter III, Section 2) engendered by their use are taken into consideration. However, as we shall see, the notion of an ontological commitment is defined only for a regimented language. Hence, to show that the terms in question are not coreferential one first has to *translate* them into a canonical notation. But the fact that translation is needed makes the argument inconclusive.

The *possibility* of constructing a language which is sensitive to differences neglected by another proves to be important for the defence of another of Quine's theses, to be discussed later, namely, Ontological Relativity. On the other hand, it seems irrelevant to us in the context of the debate in which we are currently engaged.

It is clearly sophistical to pretend that the word 'uncle' is *ambiguous* in English because in Latin there exist two words, one for a maternal uncle, and one for a paternal uncle.[1] Equally, it seems unacceptable to argue that the terms 'river' and 'collection of river-stages' used by Glotzbach's speakers are inscrutable, because predicate calculus can project onto their language a distinction which is absent from it.

13. Indeterminacy of Translation, the Weaker Versus the Stronger Version

In *From a Logical Point of View* Quine was anxious to make a clear distinction between the well behaved notions of the *theory of reference* (truth, extension, reference), on the one hand, and the suspect notions of the *theory of meaning* (meaning, synonymity, analyticity), on the other. At the same time he argued for the inseparability of language and theory.

The *Indeterminacy thesis*, however, seems to conflict with both of these earlier points of view. On the one hand it tends to *weaken the contrast* between theories of meaning and of reference; each is exposed to the same dangers, since the inscrutability of reference is strictly analogous to the indeterminacy of meaning. On the other hand, Quine seems to wish to widen the gap between language and theory, since he maintains that the indeterminacy of translation is 'additional' to the underdetermination of scientific theory by data.

It is my claim that, properly assessed, the Indeterminacy thesis reduces to the claim that the distinction between correct and incorrect translation is as elusive as the distinction between *verbal disagreement* and *disagreement in belief*. Such a claim is much weaker than the position which Quine now

---

[1] I owe this to H. Hubien.

defends. Instead of saying that every translation is *relative* (to a translation manual), we simply say that the border-line between translating and embellishing the native doctrine is *fuzzy*.

Quine maintains that there is no such a thing as an *objective matter* for translators to be right or wrong about. It is enlightening to ask Quine what is missing. In his early paper "The Problem of Meaning in Linguistics" he appealed to the elusiveness of synonymy: "... pending some definition of synonymy, we have no statement of the problem; we have nothing for the lexicographer to be right or wrong about" (Quine [1953e], p. 63). In his recent *Theories and Things*, Quine appeals to a very different argument. He claims that what is missing is a physical difference underlying the difference between rival manuals of translation:

... when I say there is no fact of the matter, as regards, say, the two rival manuals of translation, what I mean is that both manuals are compatible with all the same distributions of states and relations over elementary particles. In a word, they are physically equivalent. (Quine [1981a], p. 23)

This passage might help unterstand why the indeterminacy of manuals of translation with respect to speech dispositions is worse than the underdetermination of physical theories with respect to observations. Neither indeterminacy nor underdetermination can be overcome by acquiring new data. But in one case, beyond data, there is something, namely matter. Whereas in the other case there is not a comparable entity, namely meaning. We have good grounds to posit *particles* and recognize "a dozen or so basic states and relations in which they may stand (ibid.)" but we lack reasons of the same strength to posit *meanings*. Meanings have no explanatory power, contrary to particles.

If this is what Quine has in mind, his contrast between the status of *particles* and the status of *meanings* is acceptable. Professional linguists subscribe to Quine's rejection of *meanings* conceived as entities to be captured by good translations:

The naive monolingual speaker of English (or of any other language) might be tempted to think that the meanings of lexemes (their sense and denotation) are independent of the language that he happens to speak and that translation from one language to another is simply a matter of finding the lexemes which have the same meaning in the other language, selecting the grammatically appropriate forms and putting them together in the right order. But this is not the case, as anyone who has any practical experience of translation is well aware. (Lyons [1977], 235)

There are linguistic facts, stressed by Ferdinand de Saussure, which show that meanings cannot be construed as entities detachable from language:

> The denotation of "mat" is limited by its contrast in sense with "rug" and "carpet"; the denotation of "paillasson" in French is limited by its contrast in sense with "tapis" and other lexemes. We could not reasonably say that "mat" has two meanings because it is translatable into French by means of two non-synonymous lexemes, "tapis" and "paillasson"; or that "tapis" has three meanings because it can be translated into English with three non-synonymous lexemes, "rug", "carpet", and "mat". The meanings of words (their sense and denotation) are internal to the language to which they belong. This, as far as the vocabulary of languages is concerned, is what is meant by saying that each language has its own semantic structure, just as it has its own grammatical and phonological structure. (Lyons, [1977], p. 238)

The linguistic data considered by Lyons do not only show that meanings cannot be detached from language. They also justify a more startling conclusion, namely that meanings are proper to each language rather than common to all of them ("each language has its own semantic structure").

From this however, Lyons does not infer the baffling thesis which Quine has argued for, i.e. the indeterminacy of translation. He holds that these facts make translating difficult (p. 237), not that they make it impossible or uncertain.

How is it possible for Quine to start from a fact which has been widely acknowledged by linguists since Ferdinand de Saussure, i.e. the fact that meaning is internal to language, and to reach a conclusion which no translator would subscribe to, i.e. that translation is indeterminate?

One of the reasons is this. We do not aim at translating *languages*. We aim at translating sequences of utterances as Ladmiral observes. *Languages* conceived as combinations of a lexicon and a grammar cannot be mapped onto one another, but from this *it does not follow* that *texts*, *speeches* and finite formulations of *theories* cannot be translated, except for those who fail to distinguish between languages and texts. But this is precisely a failure which can be imputed to Quine to a certain extent. One should remember his tendency to blur the distinction between *language* and *theory* which I have commented on at length in the first chapter.

Admittedly, the fact that meaning is internal to language is only one among the data which Quine relies on to support his indeterminacy thesis. He also brought more original considerations to bear on the issue such as the multiple ways of mapping sets of holophrastic sentences one onto the other using rival ways of dismembering these sentences. Or by appeal to the principle of *charity* which recommends that we explain away absurd beliefs as bad translations.

Neither of these arguments, however, establishes the indeterminacy thesis in the strong sense.

The first one is an enthymeme whose missing premiss is highly questionable (language and theory formulation cannot be separated from one another). The second one ignores the constraints of surface syntax whilst the third one only supports the *weaker* version of the indeterminacy thesis.

III
Ontology

1. The Critique of the Linguistic Conception of Ontology

The importance and originality of "Two Dogmas of Empiricism" stems from the fact that Quine mounts a frontal attack on the doctrine of analyticity, which occupied a central position in neo-positivist philosophy, whilst remaining faithful to Empiricism and to the idea of unified science professed by members of the Vienna Circle. Moreover, Quine's attack on analyticity was part of a more important attack on the linguistic conception of logical truth, subscribed to by Carnap and others. But Carnap did not just subscribe to a linguistic conception of logical truth. He also subscribed to a linguistic, even conventionalist, conception of ontology, at least in the philosophical sense of the word.

Carnap made this point in a particularly clear way in "Empiricism, Semantics, and Ontology":

And now we must distinguish two kinds of questions of existence: first, questions of the existence of certain entities of the new kind *within the framework*; we call them *internal questions*; and second, questions concerning the existence or reality *of the system of entities as a whole*, called *external questions* ...
... Let us consider as an example the simplest [framework] dealt with in the everyday language: the spatio-temporally ordered system of observable things and events. Once we have accepted the thing language with its framework for things, we can raise and answer internal questions, e.g. "Is there a white piece of paper on my desk?", "Did King Arthur actually live?", "Are unicorns and centaurs real or merely imaginary?" and the like. These questions are to be answered by empirical investigations.
From these questions we must distinguish the external question of the reality of the thing world itself. (Carnap [1950], p. 206–207)

Now for Carnap an external question is not a question about reality, the answer to which would be a scientifically testable conjecture. It is rather a question about language which calls for a *decision*; it is, he writes, "... a matter of a practical decision concerning the structure of our language". (Carnap [1950], p. 207)

In Carnap's view the traditional questions of metaphysics are badly formulated. In place of an ontological question which was *implicitly* about the world, e.g., "Do things (as opposed to sense-data) exist?", Carnap recommends the substitution of a question that is *explicitly* about language, namely, "Are we interested in using a thing-language rather than a sense-datum language?"

Many of the elements of this view were present in his earlier work *The Logical Syntax of Language*. But there are two important differences between this early work and his later position. In the early work he recommended translation of metaphysical questions into the formal mode which was a syntactic metalanguage, whereas the translations envisaged in the later work are into a semantic metalanguage. Secondly, at least some of the statements of ontology are no longer treated as nonsense, but rather as linguistic conventions in the material mode.

Now Quine attacks the linguistic conception of ontology defended by Carnap with as much vigour as he has attacked the linguistic conception of logical truth. Moreover, there is a tight connection between the two Carnapian doctrines which is the prime target of both of Quine's critiques. Quine himself makes an allusion to this connection, which we shall explain later, in these terms:

Though no one has influenced my philosophical thought more than Carnap, an issue has persisted between us for years over questions of ontology and analyticity. These questions prove to be interrelated ... (Quine [1951b], p. 203)

Whereas Carnap has banished statements of general ontology from science, Quine sets out to restore Ontology to its traditional position as a discourse about reality (what there is), in contrast to a discourse just about language; whilst at the same time recognizing, apparently paradoxically, that Carnap and the logical empiricists were right to stress the metalinguistic nature of ontological statements. Quine does not recommend a return to a conception of Ontology as a direct study of *being*, or *reality*. He does not consider the 'linguistic turn', seen by Ayer as a 'revolution in philosophy', to be a passing episode during which the real problems of ontology are momentarily eclipsed by less interesting ones about language. On the contrary. He places general ontology on the same level with natural science not by *playing-down* the importance of linguistic considerations in metaphysics, but rather by *stressing* the importance of their role in science.

Thus the last chapter of *Word and Object* has the provocative title "Semantic Ascent".

Quine also bridges the gap between general ontology and science by uncovering a theoretical import in the choice of linguistic frameworks:

The quest of a simplest, clearest overall pattern of canonical notation is not to be distinguished from a quest of ultimate categories, a limning of the most general traits of reality. (Quine [1960a], p. 161)

In Quine's view the ontologist ought not to begin his inquiry with questions formulated in the so-called material-mode, such as 'What objects (particulars, universals, or what not) are there?' A detour through language is inevitable; so that the first question the ontologist ought to ask is 'What does a theory say there is?', a question that is quite clearly a *semantic* one. Only then can he go on to ask the traditional question of epistemology 'What theories ought we to adopt?' And it is from the answer to this question and the preceding one that he will derive an answer to the *ontological* question 'What is there?' The *semantic* inquiry is the part of this work on which philosophers have the most to say, since the *epistemological* question ('What theory should we adopt?') is passed over to the scientist. As Bonevac observes:

The latter question can be treated by philosophers only in a very general way, since we adopt theories for a wide variety of reasons, varying according to subject matter. What physical theory we should adopt, for example, is properly a question for the physicist to decide; which account of the French Revolution we should accept is best adjudicated by the historian. (Bonevac [1980], p. 229–230)

Quine, *qua* philosopher, is therefore especially interested in the semantic stage of the ontological inquiry.

2. The Criterion of Ontological Commitment

Quine's criterion of ontological commitment is not simply meant to tell us what entities a given theory *says* there is; its aim is rather to detect what entities a theory is *committed* to. And this is not a trivial task, which could be solved simply by asking which explicit existence statements, (that is, statements that *assert* the existence of something), occur in the theory.

For just as a logician may accept as true a set of axioms which, unknown to him, contain a contradiction – so can someone, without knowing it, commit himself to the existence of certain entities. The utility of a criterion of ontological commitment is thus the same as that of a geiger-counter; it enables one to detect hidden commitments, just as the geiger-counter enables one to detect radiations that are not ordinarily perceptible.

Many arguments developed in the Middle Ages during the celebrated quarrel over universals now appear sterile. One of the causes of this sterility could well have been the fact that a criterion of ontological commitment was lacking at that time. Church has underlined the importance of such a criterion: "... no discussion of an ontological question, in particular of the issue between nominalism and realism, can be regarded as intelligible unless it obeys a definite criterion of ontological commitment". (Church [1958], p. 1012)

The merit of having formulated such a criterion belongs to Quine. And since he is reluctant to draw a clear distinction between language and theory, it is not surprising that he should have hesitated for a long time over deciding whether the object to which the criterion in question applies is a language or a theory.

One of the first formulations of the criterion goes back to 1939. In "A Logistical Approach to the Ontological Problem" Quine writes: "We may be said to countenance such and such an entity if and only if we regard the range of our variables as including such an entity." (Quine [1939a], p, 199) And in the same year, in "Designation and Existence", he attributes ontological commitments to languages: "In realistic languages, variables admit abstract entities as values; in nominalistic languages they do not." (Quine [1939b], p. 50)

Later, in "Logic and the Reification of Universals" (1953) he attributes ontological commitments to theories:

In general, *entities of a given sort are assumed by a theory if and only if some of them must be counted among the values of the variables in order that the statements affirmed in the theory be true.* (Quine [1953c], p. 103)

And, he continues, opportunely underlining the difference between a criterion of ontological commitment and an ontological assertion: "I am not suggesting a dependence of being upon language. What is under consideration is not the ontological state of affairs, but the ontological commitments of a discourse." (Quine [1953c], p. 103)

This warning will prevent some people from being misled by the elliptical formulation 'To be is to be the value of a variable'. The criterion of ontological commitment does not reveal what *is*, as Berkeley's criterion *Esse est percipi* was meant to, but tells us only what a scientific discourse or a theory *says* there is. Quine himself has drawn attention to this point: "We look to bound variables in connection with ontology not in order to know what there is, but in order to know what a given remark or doctrine, ours or someone else's, *says* there is ..." (Quine [1948], p. 15)

We should also bear in mind that Quine's criterion applies to scientific theories forced into the predicate calculus as opposed to theories formulated in natural language or in functor logic. For those who accept Quine's criterion the latter formulations are not *free* from ontological commitments, they simple *conceal* them.

We said earlier that often someone is unaware of the ontological commitments of a theory that he accepts, and that a test is therefore needed to detect them. This clearly shows that the set of a theory's *ontological commitments* does not coincide with the set of *existence statements* belonging to the theory. For whilst the latter are explicit, the former may not be. What then is the difference between the two classes?

At first sight a plausible explanation equates 'ontological commitment' with 'existential presupposition'. This suggestion gains support from certain passages of Quine's in which he speaks of 'presupposed objects' or of *the entities that a given theory presupposes* (Quine [1951b], p. 206) in contexts in which ontological assumptions are in question. Thus, one is led quite naturally to ask whether 'commitment' for Quine means the same as 'presupposition' does for Frege and Strawson. If this were so, then the *negation* of a statement *would carry* the same ontological commitments as does its assertion *just as* $\sim p$ *carries the same presupposition as p*. In other words, the statement 'Something is a dog' which has the form

(1) $(\exists x)(Ax)$

would, if this were so, involve the same ontological assumptions as the statement 'Nothing is a dog', which is of the form

(2) $\sim (\exists x)(Ax)$,

and which, in turn, is logically equivalent to

(3) $(\forall x)(\sim Ax)$[1]

This plausible interpretation of the notion of 'commitment' has been advanced by Hintikka:

> What he [Quine] appears to mean is that a sentence is committed to the existence of all the values of the bound variables it contains, not just to the existence of those specific values (if any) which are needed to make the sentence true. In short, $(\exists x) A(x)$ and $(\forall x) \sim A(x)$ carry the same ontic commitments. (Hintikka [1968], p. 79)

Quine, however, has rejected this interpretation:

> My remaining remark aims at clearing up a not unusual misunderstanding of my use of the term 'ontic commitment'. The trouble comes of viewing it as my key ontological term, and therefore identifying the ontology of a theory with the class of all things to which the theory is ontically committed. This is not my intention. (Quine [1968c], p. 287)

In other words, $(Ex) A(x)$ and $(\forall x) \sim A(x)$ share the same ontology, i.e., the same domain of variables, but not the same ontological commitment. Uttering the sentence (1) commits the speaker to dogs, whereas uttering the sentence (2) or (3) commits him only to a non-empty universe (in virtue of standard first order logic, which is not a free logic).

Quine's reply to Hintikka clearly shows that 'ontological commitment' should not be understood as presupposition but rather as 'implication'. We side with Gottlieb who writes:

> ... the most defensible criterion of ontological commitment [reads as follows]: T is ontologically committed to a if and only if, T logically implies $(\exists x)(x = a)$, [and to F's if and only if T logically implies $(\exists x)(Fx)$]. (Gottlieb [1980], p. 41)

Gottlieb's solution was anticipated by Church who says that

> [a theory T is committed to] M's if and only if, '$(\exists x)(Mx)$' is a theorem of T. (Church [1958], p. 1009)

---

[1] We have adopted the policy of uniformizing the notation. Universal quantifiers which Quine and many other authors used to represent by a variable between parentheses (for instance '(x)') are now represented by variables preceded by '$\forall$'. We have replaced Hintikka's 'E' by '$\exists$'.

The implication in question is logical implication as opposed to material implication. Material implication is too weak, so that construing 'implies' as 'materially implies', would have unintuitive consequences, which Chihara has indicated. Here is one:

> Another unintuitive consequence is connected with the fact that '$(\forall x)(x$ is a ghost $\supset x$ is a unicorn)' is a true sentence. A theory affirming '$(\exists x)(x$ is a ghost)' would thus be ontologically committed to unicorns. (Chihara [1973], p. 102)

3. Is the Predicate 'x is committed to y' Extensional?

Several authors (Scheffler and Chomsky, A.R. Anderson) have pointed out that the dyadic 'x is ontologically committed to y' cannot be construed as a well-behaved extensional relation without imputing to whoever *describes* the ontological commitments of a theory those very commitments, even when the author of the description does not *subscribe* to what he describes.

Suppose that a theory entails

(4) $(\exists x)(x$ is a unicorn).

How shall we describe this ontological commitment? If we write

(5) $(\exists x)(x$ is assumed by (4) and x is a unicorn),

we incur the obligation of sharing that ontological commitment. But this is counter-intuitive, as Quine himself admits:

> So long as I adhere to my ontology, as opposed to McX's, I cannot allow my bound variables to refer to entities which belong to McX's ontology and not to mine. (Quine [1948], p. 16)

However, Quine himself proposed a solution to this difficulty; it consists in ascending to the metalinguistic level:

> I can, however, consistently describe our disagreement by characterizing the statements which McX affirms. (Quine [1948], p. 16)

Scheffler and Chomsky propose to solve the problem in the same way: they move in Carnap's parlance to 'the formal mode of speech'. The following schema enables them to construct an indefinitely large number of specific criteria of ontological commitments which enable the commentator to avoid ontological commitments of the theory he describes.

(6) T makes a —— -assumption if and only if it yields a statement of the form '$(\exists x)(x$ is (a) ——$)$' (Scheffler and Chomsky [1958–1959], p. 79)

For example

(7) T makes a unicorn-assumption if and only if it yields a statement of the form '$(\exists x)(x$ is a unicorn)'.

The trouble with the solution is that the schematic positions marked by blanks (——) are opaque (see Chapter VII, Section 1) hence we cannot do justice to the logical potential of complex ontological commitments[1]. Hence we cannot account for the fact that whoever is committed to unicorns and centaurs is also committed to unicorns.

We have dealt with the claim that 'x ontologically commits us to y' is an intentional predicate[2] like 'x seeks y'. Let us now come to grips with the claim that it is intensional.

Suppose someone advocates a theory which commits him to the existence of *renates*. Shall we say that he is also committed to the existence of *cordates*? An affirmative answer will lead to the counter-intuitive consequences disclosed by Chihara. A negative answer seems to force on Quine the recognition that the the concept of ontological commitment is an intensional one. To break through the horns of this dilemma, and to give a fully satisfactory answer to the former difficulty as well, one has to take a crucial step, i.e., one has to formalize the criterion of ontological commitment.

---

[1] This point is made in B. Taylor's M.A. thesis in connection with a treatment similar to that of Scheffler and Chomsky.
[2] A mental act is intentional if it is directed at or about an object which is not necessarily a real or existent thing (seeking Pegasus). A predicate is intentional if it expresses an intentional mental act.

4. B. Taylor's Formalization of the Criterion of Ontological Commitment

The predicate 'x is ontologically committed to y' is a semantic predicate. We got into trouble when we tried to conceive of it as the expression of a relation between linguistic entities and extralinguistic entities. This kind of problem has already been solved by Tarski for other semantic predicates such as 'X is true' or 'X satisfies Y'. As Rogers observes

> First, one may introduce [semantical terms] by DEFINING them all in terms of the specifically non-semantical terms already available in one's metalanguage M. (R. Rogers [1963], p. 52)

Commenting on the merits of this policy, he adds:

> A strong argument in favor of it is that by defining all one's semantical terms exclusively in terms of non-semantical terms, one has a kind of guarantee that the paradoxes associated with the use of semantical terms will not appear in one's metalanguage .... (R. Rogers [1963], *ibid*)

B. Taylor has taken this line in his unpublished M.A. thesis, about ontological commitment. To formulate the ontological commitments of a theory expressed in a logistic system L (which contains at least the first-order predicate calculus with identity), he begins by introducing

> ... an extensional semantical metalanguage SML of L containing a truth-predicate 'Tr' which fulfils Tarski's criterion of adequacy, convention T ... and in which the values of the variables of L are interpreted as being objects in some domain. (Taylor [1970], p. 41)

then he reminds us that semantical terms can be eliminated altogether:

> If ... SML contains variables of a higher order than those of L, it is possible to introduce semantical expressions by definition; thus SML need contain no semantical part, in our present sense, provided it is sufficiently rich. (Taylor [1970], p. 44)

Let us assume that SML contains the following metalinguistic predicates which are definable in SML:

Exp (x),   i.e., x is an expression.

Pr (x),   i.e., x is provable.

Tr (x),   i.e., x is true.

$P_D(y)$,   i.e., y is a value in the domain D.

The domain of SML will contain linguistic entities, but also the extra-linguistic entities which belong to the domain of L, i.e., the elements of the domain of L of which 'P_D' is true.

With this apparatus Taylor put forward several partial formalizations of the criterion of ontological commitment. Let us concentrate on the second one (A^2):

(A^2) ... entities y which are members of $\{x: Ax\}$ are assumed by L iff $(\forall x)$ $(\text{Exp}(x) \to (\text{Pr}(x) \to \text{Tr}(x))). \to . (\exists y)(P_D(y) \& y \varepsilon \{n: Ax\})$. (Taylor [1971], p. 51)

which, in the vernacular, reads as follows: ... entities y which are members of the set of A's are assumed by theory L if and only if the theorems (i.e. the expressions which, if provable are true) of L logically imply that there exists something in the domain D and that it is an A.

This tentative formalization however, falls prey to the very objection which Scheffler and Chomsky raised against the naïve formulation:

... to accept as true the truths of SML, including the right hand side of (A^2), involves sharing commitment to the domain of L. (Taylor [1970], p. 54)

To meet this objection, Taylor moves one step higher in the 'semantic ascent', i.e., he rewrites (A^2) as (A^3):

(A^3) ... entities y which are members of $\{x: Ax\}$ are assumed by L iff $\vdash_{\text{SML}} (\forall x)$ $(\text{Exp}(x) \to (\text{Pr}(x) \to \text{Tr}(x))). \to . (\exists y)(P_D(y) \& y \varepsilon \{x: Ax\})$. (Taylor [1970], p. 55)

i.e., he moves to the syntactic metalanguage of SML, "whose domain is just the set of expressions of SML" (Taylor, ibid.), that is to say, a domain which anybody is prepared to countenance.

One might fear that the left hand side of the definition still carries an unwanted ontological commitment but here again, the metalinguistic ascent helps us out of trouble. The final formulation which emerges is the following in which the word 'entities' is not *used* but *mentioned*.

($\exists^1$) '$\vdash_{SML} (\forall x) (\text{Exp}(x) \to (\text{Pr}(x) \to \text{Tr}(x))). \to . (\exists y) (P_D(y) \& y\varepsilon\{x:Ax\})$'

explicates

'entities y which are members of $\{x: A(x)\}$ are assumed by a sentence s of L'. (Taylor [1970], p. 59)

On this account, the sentence

(8) 'your theory is committed to phlogiston'

has to be rephrased by,

(9) It is a theorem of the semantic metalanguage of your theory that if all of its theorems are true then there is some stuff which is phlogiston.

Let us mention here that Taylor demonstrates as a theorem that a provable sentence s of a theory L is ontically committed to any entity to which L is committed, i.e., it shares its ontic commitment with s' iff s' is a theorem of s. In other words, if s' is a sentence formulable in the theory, but not provable in the theory, its ontological commitment does not add up to that of the theorem. Hence a theory can be ontically committed to the existence of renates without being ontically committed to the existence of cordates. Yet it is possible to accommodate the latter commitments at another level; namely, that of secondary commitments:

primary ontic commitments entail secondary ontic commitments only if the premisses needed to make the inference are true on the basis of (extensional) semantical rules. (Taylor [1970], p. 88)

Hence Taylor's account circumvents the objection that the notion of ontological commitment is intensional, without being led to counter-intuitive consequences. Intensionality is reduced to the innocuous opacity of quotes required by the semantic and syntactic ascent.

5. Vuillemin's Objection to the Criterion of Ontological Commitment

Vuillemin maintains that Quine's criterion does not provide us with *necessary* conditions of an ontological commitment, but only with a *sufficient* condition, so that there are, according to him, non-quantified expressions that carry an ontological commitment.

Consider the following two statements involving asymmetrical relations:

(10) $(\exists R)$ (R is asymmetric)[1]

(11) $(\exists x)(\exists y)$ (x is to the left of y).

According to Quine, only (10), which involves a relational predicate – in this case a predicate-variable – in a *substantive* position is ontologically committed to the existence of relations. By contrast, (11) which involves the predicate-constant 'to the left of' in an *attributive* position, carries no ontological commitment to the existence of relations. Vuillemin disputes this discrimination. For him, as for the early Russell, (11) carries an ontological commitment *of the same kind* as does (10). In support of this conclusion he advances the following argument:

Consider the relation 'x is to the left of y'. Now suppose that all the ontology implied by our statement is absorbed by the individuals x and y, as we ... supposed was the case when we said that "x and y are red". On this supposition the *order* in which the individuals x and y occur in the statement should be immaterial, barring the supposition that this order is involved in their nature as individuals, ... so that one does not escape a dilemma: either the relations are external, and ordering individuals which are themselves extraneous to that order, they introduce into the universe something that is not reducible to particulars. Or else they are internal, but it is then necessary to account for the asymmetric character of the order, by making it the property of each individual itself (monadism), or the property of the collectivity of individuals (monism); but, in each case, one loses the sense of the order that is fundamental for the determination of asymmetry. (Vuillemin [1971], p. 46)

To do full justice to Vuillemin's objection, let us spell it out in formal terms. For that purpose, let us consider the statements (10) and (11) while keeping in mind Quine's views on predication. According to Quine, (10) implies (12), but is not compatible with (13), whilst (11) is compatible with (13), but does not imply (12):

---

[1] i.e. there is a relation R such that R is asymmetric.

(12) $(\exists R)(\exists a)(\exists b)\ Rab$

and

(13) $\sim(\exists R)(\exists a)(\exists b)\ Rab.$

Now Quine, we know, refuses to quantify over predicates, because to do so would result in a sentence that was not well formed: "Predicates are not names; predicates are the other parties to predication" (Quine [1970c], p. 27–28). To obtain a well formed formula it is necessary, therefore, to give R the syntactical status of a name or variable. So (10) and (11) have to be rewritten respectively as

(14) $(\exists R)\langle a, b\rangle \varepsilon R$ [1]

and

(15) $\sim(\exists R)\langle a, b\rangle \varepsilon R.$

But if it is true that only (14) is committed to the existence of relations, both (14) and (15) are committed to the existence of ordered pairs, since in each an ordered pair is located in subject position. But classes are necessary to explain the notion of an ordered pair, thus:

(16) $\langle a, b\rangle = \{\{a\}, \{a, b\}\}$ [2].

It follows then that even (15) is committed to the existence of abstract entities, classes. It seems natural to conclude from this that the criterion of ontological commitment fails to detect a *difference* which is important on Quine's standards, particularly since it is an *extensional* one. It is clear that Vuillemin wins the first round.

To answer Vuillemin's objection, one has to look beyond Quine's theories of predication, canonical notation and ontological commitment, one has to bring yet another of his theories to bear on the issue, namely the

---

[1] i.e. there is a relation R such that the ordered pair whose members are the individuals a and b is a member of R.
[2] i.e. the ordered pair of a and b is identical with the class whose members are the class having a as unique member and the class having a and b as members.

theory of virtual classes and relations which he developed in the first pages of *Set Theory and Its Logic*.

The starting point of the theory is the law of concretion:

(17) $y\varepsilon\{x: Fx\} \equiv Fy$ [1].

On the left of (17) we have the expression '$\{x: Fx\}$' which occupies what looks like the place of a name, and therefore a position that seems to be accessible to quantification. By contrast, on the right of the biconditional in (17) there is an expression that is *almost* homologous, (though not completely since 'F' contains an implicit copula), which, *qua* predicate, does not occupy a position accessible to quantification and which, therefore, carries no ontological commitment. Now Quine notes that there is a way of parsing the sentence '$y\varepsilon\{x: Fx\}$' which removes the appearance that '$\{x: Fx\}$' occupies a position that is accessible to quantification. This consists of treating '$\varepsilon\{x: Fx\}$' as a unitary expression which cannot be further decomposed. In other words, instead of construing 'ε' as a dyadic predicate and '$\{x: Fx\}$' as a class abstract, he construes '$\varepsilon\{x: Fx\}$' as a monadic predicate.

Now this treatment of class abstracts can be extended to relation abstracts. Quine points out that

Just as the law of concretion for classes was used ... to provide a joint definition of membership and class abstraction, so the law of concretion for relations provides a joint definition of the attribution and abstraction of relations: '$z\{xy: Fxy\} w$' for 'Fzw'. (Quine [1963a], p. 21)

In other words, the following equivalence

(18) $\langle zw \rangle \varepsilon\{xy: Fxy\} \equiv z\{xy: Fxy\} w \equiv Fzw$,

shows that polyadic predicates do not raise a *special* problem for Quine.

Polyadic predicates do not carry *more* ontological commitment than monadic predicates and consequently Vuillemin's *argument* fails to establish that predicates carry ontological commitment on their own. But Vuillemin's *thesis* – as opposed to his *argument* – remains unaffected. Quine owes us a justification for his decision to locate reference in bound variables

---

[1] i.e. y is a member of the class of all x which are F if and only if y is F.

in subject position, so that predicates in predicate position have no reference (see also Berka [1983]).

Are there *independent* reasons for the claim that predicates do not refer? To answer this question, we have to go deeper into the matter and scrutinize the syntactic and semantic status of predicates.

6. The Syntactic and Semantic Status of Predicates

As we have seen before (p. 77) Quine observes that predicates are not names. He also observes that sentences are not names. In accordance with these observations, he dismisses the quantification of predicates as it is exemplified in the formula

(19) $(\exists x)(\exists F) Fxy$,

and the quantification of sentences as it is exemplified in the formula

(20) $(p)(p \lor \sim p)$.

Quine's position departs from the traditional one in both cases. Quantification over the predicates already appears in Aristotle and in his early commentator Ammonius. The Pseudo-Scotus, on the other hand, allows for propositions in which the predicate is 'a common name preceded by a universal sign' (though this does not commit him to believing that such expressions as *nullum animal* are themselves names) (P. Thom [1982], p. 142; see also P. Thom [1981]; see also L. Hickman [1980]).

On the other hand, to mention a much more recent tradition Lewis and Langford currently quantify over sentences.

At this stage, Quine, as I understand him, rejects the quantification of predicates and sentences on *syntactic grounds*. On this point the canonical notation of the classical predicate calculus agrees with a natural language like English. In English predicates and sentences do not belong to the same syntactic category as names, at least if we adopt Lesniewski's criterion, and say that two expressions belong to the same syntactic category if and only if they are interchangeable *salva congruitate*, i.e., without generating ill-formedness. Now, it is clear that we cannot substitute the indefinite pronoun 'something' for an intransitive verb, i.e., for what logicians call a 'predicate', or for a sentence, as the following examples show:

(21) John sings.
*John something.

(22) John knows that snow is white.
*John knows that something.

Admittedly one may say:

(23) John does something,

and,

(24) John knows something,

but in the first case one has to split 'sings' into 'sings a song', and in the second case, one quantifies over a nominalized sentence ('*that* snow is white'), not over a sentence.

Although Quine dismisses the use of predicate variables or sentential variables, he allows the use of predicate schematic letters, or of sentence schematic letters. Schematic letters can be replaced by constants and capture what is shared by all constants of the same syntactic category. For instance:

(25) $p \vee \sim p$

captures what is common to

(26) a) it rains or it does not rain
b) $2 + 2 = 4$ or $2 + 2 \neq 4$
c) .... or .... not ......

Unlike variables, however, schematic letters cannot be bound by a quantifier.

This piece of legislation should not be seen as a way of banning higher order logic. Higher order logic can be recast into the idiom of set theory. Instead of writing

(27) $(\exists x)(\exists F) Fx$,

we can write

(28) $(\exists x)(\exists \alpha) x \varepsilon \alpha$,

where 'ε' plays the role of the predicate.

Let us now turn to semantics and see what status Quine gives to predicates and to sentences. For Quine the bearers of reference are bound variables in subject-position and nothing else. But though predicates have no reference this does not prevent them from being *meaningful*. A linguistic expression can occur as an essential part of a meaningful sentence without being a name. Prepositions, conjunctions, articles, commas, are cases in point. The latter expressions are commonly classified as *syncategorematic expressions*. (Quine [1939a], p. 197)

Are predicates syncategorematic as well? In his early paper 'A Logistical Approach to the Ontological Problem' Quine divided the class of meaningful expressions into two exclusive and jointly exhaustive subsets: names and syncategorematic expressions. If we stick to this account, predicates are syncategorematic. Predicates do not *refer*. Here Quine anticipates Ryle in rejecting the 'Fido'-Fido theory applied to predicates. Quine confines the predicates to the role of contributing to meaning as opposed to reference. Predicates cannot refer, but they can be meaningful.

Later, in *Word and Object*, Quine, probably influenced by Tarski, gives predicates status not only in the ill-behaved theory of meaning but also in the well-behaved theory of reference. Although he still maintains that predicates *do not refer* to classes or properties, he recognizes that they are *true of* or *false of* (*satisfied by* to use Tarski's word) the objects referred to by singular terms (names or bound variables).

Küng, however, objects that this account fails to answer the following question: "... why is a certain predicate sign true for some individuals and not for others?" (Küng [1967], p. 156). One might be tempted to reply that the predicate 'F' is *true of* the objects $a_1 \ldots a_n$ because $a_1 \ldots a_n$ share the property F. But this is really an unsatisfactory answer since we do not have independent access to properties and we content ourselves with positing a property for each predicate. At this stage, although we are not doing *bad semantics*, – i.e., we do not say that predicates *refer to* properties – we are nevertheless doing *bad metaphysics*, i.e., we are inferring the existence of properties from the existence of predicates – a very dubious inference indeed which rests on the picture-theory of language.

Quine, however, could answer Küng's question *without positing properties*. He could, and would say, that the predicate '*F*' is true of the objects $a_1 \ldots a_n$ in virtue of *its meaning*. One should observe, here, an important shift. The answer to Küng's question is not given within the theory of reference, but within the theory of meaning.

Küng dissmissed the answer we are suggesting on the grounds that Quine ascribes meaning to units larger than predicates alone, and even sentences: "... even an entire sentence [according to Quine] is meaningless if taken in isolation; only the totality of sentences asserted by science can be said to be meaningful".[1] (Küng [1967], p. 158)

Küng's criticism would be fatal to the answer I propounded if Quine had stuck to the holistic theory of meaning defended in *Two Dogmas*, but he has not. As we have seen, Quine provided a much more elaborated semantics in *Word and Object*. This semantics allows occasion observation sentences to be *meaningful* in *isolation*. Moreover predicates can also be meaningful in isolation, once we have *abstracted* their satisfaction-conditions with the help of analytical hypotheses.

It is important to observe here that we can spell out the satisfaction conditions of first order predicates *without* committing ourselves to classes or properties, i.e., without quantifying over classes and properties. All we need to do is to quantify over individuals. For instance, the satisfaction-conditions for the predicate '*x* is a prime number' can be given, as Romanos observes ([1983], p. 162) by the clause

(29) For all *a*, *a* satisfies '*x* is a prime number' if and only if *a* is a prime number.

We are not compelled to say,

(30) For all *a*, *a* satisfies '*x* is a prime number' if and only if there is a class of prime numbers to which *a* belongs.

Polyadic predicates seem, at first sight to create a problem. It looks as if the formulation of their satisfaction-conditions requires quantification over ordered *n*-tuples. This is not so, however. The satisfaction conditions of '*x* is bigger than *y*' can be given by the clause:

---

[1] It remains true, however, that the *ultimate* and *clearest* meaning bearers are scientific theory as a whole at one extreme and observation sentences at the other. The truth bearers are each of the sentences asserted in the theory. Holism applies to meaning, not to truth.

(31)   For all *a* and *b* where *b* is followed by *a*, *a* and *b* satisfy '*x* is bigger than *y*' if and only if *a* is bigger than *b*.

We are not forced to say:

(32)   For all ordered pairs ⟨*a*, *b*⟩, ⟨*a*, *b*⟩ satisfies '*x* is bigger than *y*' if and only if *a* is bigger than *b*.

First order predicates do not *refer* to properties or classes but are *satisfied* by individuals. The semantic relation of satisfaction, however, can be viewed as a kind of relation of reference: divided as opposed to undivided reference. Quine made this clear in *Word and Object*. He distinguishes several *modes of referring*.

Or, consider 'shoe', 'pair of shoes', and 'footwear': all three range over exactly the same scattered stuff, and differ from one another solely in that two of them divide their reference differently and the third not at all. (Quine [1960a] p. 91).

Hence we cannot criticize Quine for arbitrarily denying reference to predicates or for ignoring the contribution of predicates to the ontological commitment of sentences. Both criticisms are misguided. Quine grants a certain sort of reference to predicates and he gives an alternative formulation of the criterion of ontological commitment in terms of predicate satisfaction (see Quine [1969] p. 95 and Lauener's elaboration in Lauener [1982] p. 129).

7. Quine and the Traditional Problem of Universals, Trapp's Criticism

Does Quine's canonical notation remain neutral with respect to the problem of universals, as formulated in the philosophical tradition? Trapp argues that it is not. He introduces a very useful distinction between *extensive* and *intensive* ontology (Trapp [1976], pp. 110–117): the former deals with the sort of values we quantify over (individual variables, class variables, property variables, proposition variables), the latter is concerned with the status we give to the classes, properties or propositions we quantify over. Trapp argues that Quine's criterion does not help us with the second problem.

For instance, if it can be shown that mathematics requires quantification over classes, we are not, however, forced to conclude that Extensionalistic Platonism is implied by science. We are free to admit quantification over classes and yet avoid Platonism at the next stage, i.e., when coming to grips with the problem of the *nature* of classes which belongs to *intensive* ontology. We could, for instance, adopt Russell's *No class theory* or else a conceptualistic theory.

Contrary to the Platonistic intensive ontology which treats universals as entities belonging to a realm of ideas independent of consciousness, "a conceptualistic alternative interpretation would avoid Platonism and get away with merely two realms of entities, the physical entities and the mental entities" (Trapp [1976], p. 110). The idea is that universals are not independent entities existing *per se*, but only accidents of substances abstracted by the mind. Quine's conceptual tools ignore this issue, Trapp says, and in this respect they fail to deal with an essential problem of ontology. (Trapp [1976], p. 111)

I fully agree with Trapp's contention that Quine deals only with extensive ontology but I do not think that this is a weakness. I shall argue that the traditional problems which Trapp mentions can be discussed within the framework of extensive ontology. Russell's *No-class theory* has been proved to be a pyrrhic victory over universals because it makes use of attributes, i.e., Russell simply switched from extensional Platonism to intensional Platonism. As to the conceptualistic account of universals, Russell argued that it fails when confronted with infinite sets. Thinking of infinity cannot be explained in psychological terms. As J. Vuillemin puts it, formulating Russell's position:

> [Denoting] is not a mental or psychological relationship between the concept and the denoted object, since, precisely, in the only case in which the concept is necessary, i.e., in the infinity case, the multiplicity of the denoted object outruns the power of our mind. (Vuillemin [1968], p. 83)

In the spirit of Trapp's objection, one could also complain that Quine's ontological criterion cannot express the ontological commitment which *moderate realists* are prone to make. Moderate realists do not want to countenance universals as independant entities. Nor do they agree to renounce them entirely. They want to be able to accommodate the inference 'Socrates is wise, therefore Socrates is something' but *not* the inference 'Socrates is wise, therefore Socrates is some thing'. In order to capture this elusive distinction Bocheński suggests rephrasing Quine's criterion of ontological commitment in this way:

... for a property, to be is not to be a value of a variable but to *qualify the value of a variable*. (Bocheński [1956], p. 49)

A metaphysical claim underlies Bocheński's commitment, i.e., the claim that there are several *modes of being*: substances exist by themselves and properties only *in* substances. In the same vein, Waragai speaks of modes of being:

The sentence 'Socrates is something' does not force us to accept any new kind of entity like idea. It only says that Socrates is in some mode of being. (Waragai [1979], p. 43)

I concede that Quine's criterion cannot express this doctrine. It ignores it.

Quine does not want to accommodate *modes of being*. His distinction between *modes of referring* enables him to describe the semantics of predicates without positing properties. Hence the question about the mode of being of properties does not arise. Quine's *semantic* distinction makes the *ontological* distinction drawn by the Moderate Realists[1] unnecessary.

8. Has Quine Two Ontologies?

If science contained only singular statements such as 'If it rains, it is cold', it could be developed without adopting an ontology, by analysing such statements on the pattern '$A \supset B$'. But this account will not suffice for a statement such as "If a cat eats spoiled fish and sickens, it does not eat fish again" (Quine [1985], forthcoming). Here we wish to express not only a succession of events but also to *focus* on something *shared* by the successive events across time. The focussing is done by positing enduring objects, i.e. by adopting an ontology of physical individuals as values of "y".

(34) $(\forall y) (\forall t) [y$ eats spoiled fish and sickens at time $t_0 \supset (t_0 < t$ & y does not eat fish at time $t)]$

---

[1] For a defence of moderate realism see Kalinowski [1985].

As values of '*y*' in causal statements Quine adopts a domain of *bodies*. Thoroughgoing empirist that he is, he considers bodies as more fundamental than sense data, for the following reasons:

(a) ... we cannot hope to make such objects [sense data] suffice to the exclusion of physical objects. (Quine [1960a], p. 234)

(b) ... we do not need them in addition to physical objects, as means e.g. of reporting illusions and uncertainties. (Quine [1960a], p. 234–235)

(c) ... we also do not need sensory objects to account for our knowledge or discourse of physical objects themselves. (Quine [1960a], p. 235)

There are other candidates for the role of values of variables. Think of the Boyle-Mariotte law. For a perfect gas at constant temperature, the product of pressure and volume is a constant. The law can be formulated in this way:

(35) $p \times v = c$

But in a first order predicate calculus with identity, functors can be paraphrased away into predicates. The arguments of the functor, however, will recur as bound variables. Does this mean that besides quadridimensional physical objects, we are also committed to units of pressure, volume, temperature, velocity and so on?

Quine answers negatively. He avails himself of Carnap's treatment of 'impure numbers':

We are initially confronted with a theory whose objects include place-times x and impure numbers α and whose primitive predicates include 'H'. We reduce the theory to a new one whose objects include place-times and pure numbers, and whose predicates include 'H_c'. (Quine [1964], p. 217)

For example, the sentence 'x's mass = 5 grams' which carries an implicit ontological commitment to grams can be paraphrased into 'x's mass-in-grams = 5' which commits one only to numbers.

Chris Mortensen objects, however, that the latter sentence has not the same explanatory power as the former:

One might begin to make sense of why x accelerates the way it does if told that x's mass = 5 grams, because the mass 5 grams is an entity the instantiation of which confers differential causal activity on x in accordance with physical law. But what contribution could the *number* 5 make to x's behaviour, different from the contribution the number 6 makes? (Mortensen [forthcoming])

The elimination of impure numbers brings about a drastic simplification: all we need is an ontology of physical objects and of numbers. And since Quine accepts the logicist's construction of number out of sets, he ends up with the following ontology:

Our tentative ontology for science, our tentative range of values for the variables of quantification, comes therefore to this: physical objects, classes of them, classes in turn of the elements of this combined domain, and so on up. (Quine [1954], p. 244)

Quine remained faithful for more than twenty years to this ontology. But in 1976 he seemed to abandon it in favour of a hyper-pythagorean monism in "Whither Physical Objects?" It was a result in microphysics that led Quine to abandon the notion of a four dimensional physical object in favour of field theory. This result, which was reported by Heinz Post, Quine describes as follows:

Thus consider two boxes, which I shall call the east box and the west box, and two electrons, x and y. Common sense recognizes four ways in which x and y could occupy the boxes: they could both be in the east box, or both be in the west box, or x could be in the east box and y in the west, or vice versa. But statistical findings show, according to Post, that these last two apparent possibilities have to be counted as just one: the fact of x being in the east and y in the west must be identified with the seemingly opposite fact of x being in the west and y in the east. (Quine [1976c], p. 498–499)

From this it follows that the *individual electrons* cease to be the referents: "The moral is that we should think not of individual electrons x and y at all, but of states of the boxes." (Quine [1976b], p. 499)

Is it then necessary to conclude that an ontology of *individual electrons* should be replaced by one of states? The box symbolizes a region of space-time, and the states are nothing but attributes *of* regions of space-time: "We are left rather with a field theory, a theory of the distribution of states over space-time" (Quine [1976b], p. 499). Consequently, one is led to treat the regions of space-time themselves as objects: "Here, then, is one way to ontologize physicalism. The objects are the space-time regions themselves." (Quine [1976b], p. 500)

Should one then admit the states of those regions as objects as well? As long as the word 'state' only occupies the position of a *predicate*, and not that of a bound variable, this is not necessary; and the principle of economy tells us not to reify things in this way:

In this event our language will include a simple predicate representing each state, and there will be no need to recognize the states themselves as objects. (Quine [1976b], p. 500)

This point is illustrated by Quine with the following example: one of the state-predicates that will be needed is the dyadic predicate '$Fx\alpha$' which is interpreted as follows:

(36) The region α of space-time has the degree of temperature denoted by x.

In (36) the variable 'α' takes as values classes of quadruples of real numbers playing the role of cartesian coordinates, and 'x' takes real numbers denoting degrees centigrade. Now numbers can be constructed out of sets whose only member is the null set, sets of sets whose only member is the null set, etc ... Thus, the theory of sets to which the physicist appeals as an auxiliary discipline ends up by reducing physical reality itself to just one sort of entity, sets:

Finally the regions went over into pure sets; still, the set theory itself was there for no other reason than the need for mathematics as an adjunct to physical theory. (Quine [1976b], p. 503)

At this point one might object that the ontological reduction which Quine suggests is self-defeating[1]: the specification of space-time coordinates requires an *origin* given by somebody who points to a specific region of space-time. Quine concedes this:

The specificity of the coordinates would make itself known only when one descends to coarser matters of astronomy, geography, geology, and history, and here it is perhaps appropriate. (Quine [1981a], p. 18)

---

[1] I owe this objection to J.J.C. Smart.

But in the preceding sentence he claims that theoretical physics does not need to specify coordinates and minimizes the concession:

... no numerically specific coordinate will appear in the laws of truly theoretical physics, thanks to the very arbitrariness of the coordinates. (Quine [1981a], p. 18)

Here again [1], one could object that the teachings of recent cosmology seem to indicate that even the laws of theoretical physics might be time-sensitive, (the laws during the first seconds of the universe life-span are, it is claimed, different from those that hold now).

Moreover the distinction between theoretical physics and 'coarser' sciences such as astronomy, geography and geology is much too crude. Where should empirical cosmology be located? The question of whether we can leave aside specific coordinates is a serious issue in cosmology. It is related to our concept of the universe. In his *Cosmology*, Bondi writes that the universe can be defined either as "the largest set of events that can be physically linked to us" (Bondi, 1960, p. 10) or as "the largest set to which our physical laws (extrapolated in some manner or other) can be applied" (Bondi, ibid.). The second of these two definitions is more congenial to Quine's approach but it is not the one which has been adopted in the cosmologies which prevail today.

Last but not least, one might object that Quine's second ontology is too thin and that it does not seem to accommodate coarser sciences such as physiology at which level the crucial concept of *stimulation* is defined. This objection, however, is based on a serious *misunderstanding* which it is important to clear up immediately. To put it briefly, it is misleading to speak of *two* ontologies in Quine's philosophy. This formulation erroneously suggests that Quine first adopted a kind of dualism which posits physical entities and next a kind of monism which posits only empty sets and constructions thereof.

Quine's hyperpythagoreanism, however, is not an *alternative* to his physical realism. These two ontologies belong to different levels of discourse. Physical realism is the ontology Quine arrives at *from within* the scientific system of the world. Hyperpythagoreanism is the ontology he arrives at by looking at ontology *from an epistemological point of view*, i.e. by taking into account the theory of evidence and the theory of reference. The contrast holds between two *approaches* to ontology, not between two

---
[1] I owe this objection to R. Campbell.

ontologies. This will become clearer after the thesis of Ontological Relativity has been expounded (see p. 98 and p. 112).

9. Ontology, Ideology and Ontological Commitment

What remains after ontology has undergone what Quine himself describes as "a humiliating demotion"? (Quine [1983], p. 501). Has all of the reductionist programme become obsolete? Not at all. What Quine suggests is a shift from *ontological reduction* – reducing the variety of kinds of entities taken as values of our bound variables – to *ideological reduction*, i.e., the reduction which decreases the number or variety of our primitive predicates. A case in point would be the partial reduction of chemistry to physics. Reduction may consist in supplying *explicit definitions* of concepts belonging to chemistry in terms of concepts belonging to physics. But it may also consist in constructing intermediary theories devised "in order to secure a contact and a permanent improvement of the relations between the two sciences". (Lévy [1979], p. 360)

Ideological, i.e. lexical, reduction lies before us. It has not been achieved by ontological reduction to sets:

Our physical ideology remains unreduced to pure mathematics, for all the ontological debacle. (Quine [1976b], p. 503)

Hence one can understand Quine's displacement of metaphysics:

We might come to look to pure mathematics as the locus of ontology as a matter of course, and consider rather that the lexicon of natural science, not the ontology, is where the metaphysical action is. (Quine [1976b], p. 504)

So far I have tried to minimize the importance of the 'ontological debacle' by stressing the importance of ideology. I will now explore another way of making Quine's thin ontology less unpalatable.

In the passage in which Quine drew the distinction between *ontology* and *ontological commitment*, he gave the following example of the distinction:

Our question was: what objects does a theory require? Our answer is: those objects that have to be values of variables for the theory to be true. Of course a theory may, in this sense, require no objects in particular, and still not tolerate an empty universe of discourse either, for the theory might be fulfilled equally by either of two mutually exclusive universes. If for example the theory implies "($\exists x$) (x is a dog)," it will not tolerate an empty universe; still the theory might be fulfilled by a universe that contained collies to the exclusion of spaniels, and also vice versa. So there is more to be said of a theory, ontologically, than just saying what objects, if any, the theory requires; we can also ask what various universes would be severally sufficient. The specific objects required, if any, are the objects common to all those universes. (Quine [1969], p. 96)

However, this example is far from clear. It seems to suggest that if there are no hybrids, then the utterer of the sentence

(37) $(\exists x) \, \text{Dog}(x)$,

is ontologically committed to non-emptiness only.

The formalized version of the criterion of ontological commitment offered by B. Taylor makes it possible to draw the distinction between ontology and ontological commitment much more clearly: the *ontology* of a theory is made up of the entities belonging to its domain, (i.e. the entities which satisfy the predicate 'P_D'). The *ontological commitments* of a theory are made up of those entities which, additionally, are of a certain sort, i.e., the y such that $y \varepsilon P_D$ and such that $A(y/x)$, i.e. such that y satisfies the predicate Ax. Hence we can say that although physics can do with an *ontology* of pure sets, it is *ontologically committed* to those pure sets which satisfy *physical predicates*. On this view, the specification of the *ontological commitment* of a theory requires that we take into account both ontology and ideology. This means that the adoption of a hyperpythagorean ontology of pure sets would involve a *compensatory* adjustment in ideology. The distinction between mathematics and physics would remain in so far as physical predicates are not definable in terms of mathematical predicates. It would simply be *displaced*. Ideology would now bear all the weight of the distinction.

The argument leans heavily on the distinction between the domain predicate which discloses the ontology and the other predicates which express the ontological commitment, at least within B. Taylor's formal language. It is worth mentioning that the very same distinction has been formally implemented in Gupta's logical systems (Gupta [1980], p. 13). Here the domain predicate operates as a modifier which *restricts* the domain of the variable bound by the quantifier. Interestingly enough, restricted quantification in Gupta's systems *cannot* be explained away by the usual paraphrase into unrestricted quantification. For instance, 'Every K is such that if it is F, it is G', i.e. $(\forall K, x)(Fx \supset Gx)$, cannot be paraphrased into 'Anything if it is a K and if it is F, is G', i.e. into $(\forall x)(Kx \ \& \ Fx \supset Gx)$.

At the end of *Word and Object*, Quine put the ontological concern of philosophers on a par with the ontological concern of scientists.

> The question what there is is a shared concern of philosophy and most other nonfiction genres ... What distinguishes between the ontological philosopher's concern and [the zoologist's or the physicist's concern] is only the breadth of categories. (Quine [1960a], p. 275)

To interpret this passage correctly we have to appeal to the distinction between ontology and ontological commitment. The question 'What is there?' should be equated with 'What are we *ontologically committed to*?', and *not* with the question 'Which *ontology* should we choose?' The latter question has to be settled by a choice comparable with the choice of a system of coordinates. The former has not.

The right strategy for answering the question 'What is there?' consists in asking what the scientific theories to which we subscribe are ontologically committed to. Before raising this question, however, we have to prune scientific theories of unnecessary commitments by paraphrasing them in the simplest idiom. It is at this stage that Ockham's maxim should operate. For instance – to borrow an example from Chihara (1973, p. 89):

(38)   There is a difference in length between A and B

commits us to countenance differences in length but this commitment is avoidable. We can paraphrase it without loss into

(39)   A is longer than B or B is longer than A.

The ontological commitments which matter when dealing with the question of what there is are the unavoidable ones.

10. Proxy Functions

What is an avoidable ontological commitment? Clearly if we can switch from a richer ontology to a poorer one without jeopardizing the laws of the theory under consideration, we can say that the ontological commitment of the former theory was *avoidable*. We can also say that the ontology of the theory allows for a reduction. Not all reductions are acceptable. Some constraints have to be formulated. Quine introduced the notion of 'proxy function' in this context, i.e. in his attempt at characterizing acceptable ontological reduction of a theory θ to a theory θ'.

Here again Quine has forerunners. Frege invented the idea, if not the name, when he brought in the function that assigns the course of values (*Wertverlauf*) $\varepsilon f(\varepsilon)$ to every function f. The course of values *is* an object (*Gegenstand*), i.e., an entity which is one type lower than the function. It is therefore quite natural to describe this reducing function, which Frege expresses by the *spiritus lenis* as a proxy function. In his *Systeme der kumulativen Logik*, W. Degen has shown that Frege's proxy functions can be replaced in a type theoretic context by a proxy relative $A^\alpha \triangleright B^\beta$, where the type α is $>$ than type β.

Quine introduced proxy functions to provide a definition of 'ontological reduction' which rules out unwanted reductions. For instance we do not want to accept the following argument: Set theory can be regimented in first order logic. The Löwenheim-Skolem theorem states that all first order theories that have any interpretation at all, have one in the natural numbers. Therefore we need only a countable domain. Pythagorism is vindicated.

To avoid this paradoxical consequence, Quine suggested that the condition which a reduction of a theory θ to a theory θ' must meet is as follows:

We specify a function, not necessarily in the notation of θ or θ', which admits as arguments all objects in the universe of θ and takes values in the universe of θ'. This is the proxy function. Then to each n-place primitive predicate of θ, for each n, we effectively associate an open sentence of θ' in n free variables, in such a way that the predicate is fulfilled by an n-tuple of arguments of the proxy function always and only when the open sentence is fulfilled by the corresponding n-tuple of values. (Quine [1964], p. 218)

In some cases a homomorphism suffices to play the role of proxy function. Consider, for example, a theory whose domain is constituted by income tax payers and whose predicates are incapable of distinguishing between persons whose incomes are equal. In this theory, the equivalence relation 'x has the same income as y' enjoys the same substitutivity property as does the relation '$x = y$' in the background theory "in which more can be said of personal identity than equality of incomes". (Quine [1969], p. 55)

It is possible to reduce the ontology of θ, i.e., the domain D of *income tax payers*, to that of θ', i.e., to the domain D' of *incomes*. This would indisputably be a reduction, since the cardinality of D' is smaller than that of D: "The proxy function would assign to each person his income" (Quine [1969], p. 56). This proxy function is only a homomorphism, and not an isomorphism. Such a reduction is acceptable for the following reason:

... distinct persons give way to identical incomes ... [The reduction] merges the images of only such individuals as never had been distinguishable by the predicates of the original theory. (Quine [1969], p. 56)

Sometimes, however, the proxy function must of necessity be one-to-one. This will be so if the theory to be reduced is a theory about mathematical entities, the arithmetic of real numbers, for example: "This is because any two elements of such a theory are distinguishable in terms of the theory." (Quine [1969], pp. 56–57)

Consequently, if we wished to reduce the ontology of real numbers, the proxy function "would have to be one-to-one, ... to provide distinct images of distinct real numbers ..." (Quine [1969], p. 61). This requirement blocks any attempt to reduce a theory θ, whose domain is indenumerable, to a theory θ', which has a denumerable domain: "... a one-to-one mapping of an indenumerable domain into a denumerable one is a contradiction" (Quine [1969], p. 61). Therefore, the requirement that there be a proxy function rules out the possibility of basing Pythagorism on the Löwenheim-Skolem theorem. On the other hand, this requirement leaves intact those reductions that one wishes to save, such as "Frege's and Von Neumann's reduction of natural arithmetic to set theory; likewise the various essentially Dedekindian reductions of the theory of real numbers". (Quine [1964], p. 218)

The first objection that comes to mind is the following: when the proxy function must, of necessity, be one-to-one, the domain of θ' does not have a cardinality less than that of θ; one has not, therefore, effected any *economy*, but simply *changed* ontologies. For example, according to this objection, the Fregean reduction of natural numbers to classes of classes is illusory, since the *cardinality* of the set of classes of classes involved is not less than that of the natural numbers. To this objection it can be replied that the reduction is located elsewhere: the Fregean definition of number is a genuine reduction, because before Frege we needed two *kinds* of entities, sets and numbers, whereas after him we need only one. Such a reply, however, would not convince Chateaubriand who writes:

> If in ignorance of the reducibility of number theory to set theory one had adopted both theories and posited numbers and sets as distinct entities, then once one realizes that number theory is reducible to set theory one sees that it is not necessary to posit numbers and sets as distinct entities. Quine wants to say that thereby one can repudiate numbers in favor of sets. But this is misleading...
> The ontology of numbers is not repudiated at all; it is merely shown to be part of the ontology of sets. (Chateaubriand, quoted in Chihara [1973], p. 133)

Chateaubriand's riposte is not decisive. Quine could claim that Logicism accomplished a reduction in the number of *categories* of objects as opposed to a reduction in the number of *objects*.

Besides their role in the context of ontological reduction, proxy functions play an important role in the context of ontological relativity. Ontological relativity arises from the possibility of switching back and forth from one ontology to another. This is the question we shall treat next.

11. Ontological Relativity

Quine entitled one of his major works *Ontological Relativity and Other Essays*. What is the content and significance of Quine's claim that ontology is relative? How does it fit in with the other views which Quine holds? We will bring this chapter to a close by answering this question.

We have seen that as far as indeterminacy is concerned, extension and reference are not better off than intension and meaning: reference is inscrutable. In a regimented theory, i.e., a theory formulated, let us say, within the language of the predicate calculus, bound variables are the only referring expressions which survive, since Quine favours the replacement of proper names by definite descriptions which in turn are eliminated in a Russellian manner. But we have also seen that inscrutability extends to ontology: proxy functions enable us to switch from one domain for our bound variables to another, i.e., from one ontology to another, leaving the theorems unchanged. Hence ontology is relative, and ontological relativity is just a particular case of inscrutability. It is the form which inscrutability takes in a regimented theory bereft of proper names and demonstratives (indexicals).

Theoremhood remains stable while ontology varies. This is not surprising. Ontology goes with semantics, and it is well known that different interpretations can be given to the same formal system. A more interesting question, however, arises in connection with the notion of *truth*. Will truth remain stable just as much as *theoremhood*, or will it vary together with changes in ontology?

Recall, to begin with, what the theses of the inscrutability of reference and ontological relativity state respectively. The former thesis maintains that there is no absolutely correct answer to the semantic question, "Does 'rabbit' really refer to rabbits, collections of undetached parts of rabbits, etc. ...?"

When we ask, "Does 'rabbit' really refer to rabbits?" someone can counter with the question: "Refer to rabbits in what sense of 'rabbits'?" thus launching a regress; and we need the background language to regress into.

... Querying reference in any more absolute way would be like asking absolute position, or absolute velocity, rather than position or velocity relative to a given frame of reference. (Quine [1969], p. 48-49)

The latter thesis, ontological relativity, maintains that there is no absolute answer to the *ontological* question: 'Are the objects of theory T numbers, sets or bodies?' In ontology,

... there is no absolute sense in saying that all the objects of a theory [its ontology] are numbers, or that they are sets, or bodies, or something else; this makes no sense unless relative to some background theory. (Quine [1969], p. 60)

The above mentioned statements unquestionably support the claim that ontological relativity is a particular case of referential inscrutability.

An objection which might be brought against Quine at this point is that the notion of truth is defined in part in terms of that of reference so that there is surely a risk that the relativity which affects ontology might also affect truth. To this Romanos has given a decisive reply in *Quine and Analytic Philosophy*. Romanos exploits Tarski's semantic conception of truth to show that this definition of truth does not make any special assumption about the objects involved, and is to that extent *neutral*.

To begin with let us consider the partial definitions of truth obtained by substitution into convention-T,

(40) X is true in L if and only if p;

for example,

(41) '3 is a prime number' is true in English, if and only if 3 is a prime number.

It is clear that this partial definition is ontologically neutral. It explicates, i.e. eliminates, the word 'true' without making use of the suspect notion of reference, unlike the following:

(42) '3 is a prime number' is true in English if and only if the individual *referred* to by '3' is a prime number.

Moreover, the neutrality of the partial definitions extends to the general definition of truth, that is, the definition based on the concept of satisfaction. For the clauses of the *recursive definition* of the key notion of satisfaction do not make use of the notion of reference any more than do the instances of convention-T. For example, consider the following clause of the recursive definition of satisfaction:

(43) For all objects a, a satisfies 'x is a prime number' if and only if a is a prime number.

As Romanos points out,

... we are free to imagine that we are constructing different truth definitions by assuming different classes of objects quantified over in defining the satisfaction relation, but such supposedly different definitions will produce no discernible difference with respect to the total class of sentences each determines as true. Each attempt at a different account of truth will yield the same infinity of T sentences and other metalogical consequences, no matter how ontologies are switched and predicates correspondingly reinterpreted. (Romanos [1983], p. 162)

Tarski defines truth as the *satisfaction* by all sequences of objects of a sentence; but this definition is not sensitive to ontological differences between the domains of objects. It is not necessary that the various domains of objects which make a theory true should coincide; it suffices that they should be isomorphic. Truth transcends reference in the sense that it is unaffected when we change ontologies.

This point has been put decisively by Romanos:

When defining satisfaction for the expressions of a theory, then, we are free to quantify over only those domains of objects whose general structural properties permit interpretations of all the theory's predicates in their preestablished logical relations, while making all sentences of the theory come out true. (Romanos [1983], p. 163)

For Quine ontology is relative because every theory has to be interpreted against a background theory, and this in turn interpreted against another theory, and so on .... But we now know that this does not affect truth:

What matters is not what the objects of a theory are in themselves ... ; what matters is that we can determine such objects 'up to an isomorphic mapping'. Any consistent quantificational scheme will have several true interpretations. (Romanos [1983], p. 163)

Romanos' contrast between truth and ontology, however illuminating, is *one-sided*. It ignores the fact that Quine provides us with two complementary perspectives on ontology. We can look at ontology either from *within* or from *without* our system of the world. Romanos focusses on the second perspective. Quine, however, gives priority to the first one. In asking whether ontological relativity deprives the question of what there is of its factuality, he answers negatively:

I hold that actually it does not, since the question what there is is a substantive scientific question within our system of the world, whereas the point about proxy functions is a point only about evidence, a point not of ontology but of the epistemology of ontology. (Quine [1983], p. 500)

At this point, one should observe that the relativity of ontology does not 'demote' ontology, not even ontology approached *from without*, i.e., from an *epistemological* point of view. Admittedly the thesis of ontological relativity *trivializes* the difference between two alternative ontologies which can be mapped onto one another by applying a *one-to-one* transformation to the values of their variables and reinterpreting the terms of the one theory as denoting the objects of the other. The most startling example of such a trivialization is precisely the one-to-one mapping of space-time points over quadruples of real numbers which makes it possible to switch from physical realism to hyperpythagoreanism. Not all ontological choices, however, are like that for the very simple reason that it is not always possible to apply a *one-to-one* transformation to the values of the variables of the rival ontologies.

For instance, the choice between an ontology whose cardinality is $\aleph_0$ and an ontology whose cardinality is $2^{\aleph_0}$ is *not* made arbitrary by the thesis of ontological relativity. Another ontological question which remains a substantive one is the following: can we replace an ontology of real classes by an ontology of virtual classes? Quine has answered that we cannot. Last but not least one could also mention the important debate between Charles Parsons (1971) and Quine over substitutional versus objectual quantification.[1] Substitutional quantification is attractive in so far as it requires no ontology at all: variables take substituents only, i.e. they take no values. Quine argues, however, that impredicative class abstracts used as substituents of class variables contain bound class variables. To that extent they are not ontologically neutral as substituents usually are.

A problem remains, however, in so far as we are confronted with two *approaches* to ontology.

How can we reconcile the lessons of factual ontology practiced from within our scientific system of the world with the epistemological lessons taught by proxy functions? It is not enough to allocate these apparently conflicting lessons to different fields of inquiry. One should also show how they can be articulated and combined into a coherent picture. This is the aim we shall pursue in the next chapter.

---

[1] See also Orenstein (1984).

IV
Epistemology

1. The Abandonment of Foundationalism

In the short treatise *De l'art de persuader* which formulates the basic requirements of knowledge *more geometrico*, Pascal drew a useful distinction between two major tasks: the task of providing *definitions* and that of proposing *axioms*. With regard to the latter, the foundationalist programme can be stated concisely:

Don't leave any terms that are in any way unclear or equivocal without definition. Prove all propositions that are in any way obscure, employing only in their proof clearly evident axioms, or propositions already granted or proved. (Pascal [1914], p. 277)

Three centuries later, Quine formulated the foundationalist ideal in terms similar to Pascal's. In "Epistemology Naturalized" he writes:

Studies in the foundations of mathematics divide symmetrically into two sorts, conceptual and doctrinal. The conceptual studies are concerned with meaning, the doctrinal with truth. The conceptual studies are concerned with clarifying concepts by defining them, some in terms of others. The doctrinal studies are concerned with establishing laws by proving them, some on the basis of others.
... Ideally the definitions would generate all the concepts from clear and distinct ideas, and the proofs would generate all the theorems from self-evident truths. (Quine [1969], pp. 69–70)

On Quine's view, the *doctrinal part* of the foundationalist programme has not withstood attack. Gödel's first incompleteness theorem has put a final stop to the ambition of constructing a *complete* axiomatization of arithmetic. But it was Gödel's second incompleteness theorem which apparently did irreparable damage to the foundationalist program which attained its peak with Hilbert. Gödel's second theorem states that arithmetics formalized in classical logic cannot be proved consistent from within.

Yet Quine's appreciation of the situation would be judged over-pessimistic by logicians who work with relevance logic. Some of them (Meyer, Routley, McRobbie) consider that it is still an open question whether the Hilbert program could be reconstructed by using relevance logic (McRobbie 1979).[1] Since Quine does not address himself to this problem, however, we shall not pursue the matter further.

In the case of natural science the problem of induction posed by Hume opened a gap that could not be filled: "On the doctrinal side, I do not see that we are farther along today than where Hume left us." (Quine, [1969], p. 72)

Popper, though he thinks he has solved the problem of induction, rejects foundationalism.

Science does not rest upon rock-bottom. The bold structure of its theories rises, as it were, above a swamp. It is like a building erected on piles. The piles are driven down from above into the swamp, but not down to any natural or 'given' base; and when we cease our attempts to drive our piles into a deeper layer, it is not because we have reached firm ground. We simply stop when we are satisfied that they are firm enough to carry the structure, at least for the time being. (Popper, [1959], p. 111)

However, if Popper gives up all hope of founding empirical science on infallible evidence, he continues nevertheless to use the metaphor of a building. Quine goes further than Popper in this respect by rejecting the idea of a *foundation* itself. This follows clearly from the metaphor of the tottering arch that he substitutes for that of the house built on piles:

In an arch, an overhead block is supported immediately by other overhead blocks, and ultimately by all the base blocks collectively and none individually; and so it is with sentences, when theoretically fitted . . .
Perhaps we should think of the arch as tottering on an earthquake; thus even a base block is supported, now and again, only by the other base blocks via the arch. (Quine, [1960a], p. 11)

The *conceptual part* of the foundationalist programme met with partial success. Whitehead and Russell, using Frege's pioneering work, showed that all the notions of mathematics could be defined using the following three notions of logic and set theory: the Sheffer stroke, the universal

---

[1] McRobbie operates with two notions of consistency: arithmetical consistency (a theory is arithmetically inconsistent if it contains false identities among its theorems, for instance '2 = 3') and classical consistency. Inconsistent statements such as $p\ \&\ \sim p$ cause no trouble since the rule *e falso quodlibet* (formally $p\ \&\ \sim p \vdash q$) has been eliminated.

quantifier '(∀x)', and the membership predicate 'ε'. They also tried to apply this method to notions belonging to natural sciences.

But it was Carnap who took the project of attempting to provide a foundation for knowledge of the external world, further than anyone else, by rationally reconstructing the theoretical concepts of natural science in terms of observation predicates, with the help of logic and set theory. *Der logische Aufbau der Welt* [1928] is the locus classicus for that sort of endeavour. However, unlike the programme of *Principia Mathematica* [1910], even the conceptual side of Carnap's foundationalist programme came to grief. In "Testability and Meaning" [1936] he acknowledged that dispositional terms cannot be eliminated by definition, and that one is restricted to characterizing the meaning of these terms only partially by means of *reduction sentences*, for example:

(1) (∀x) [(x is placed in water) ⊃ (x is soluble ≡ x dissolves)][1]

But it can readily be seen that reduction sentences are not definitions but meaning postulates, since the main connective is a conditional rather than a biconditional. And in the *Philosophical Foundations of Physics* (1966) Carnap even gives up the idea of defining non-dispositional theoretical terms. To the question 'How, then, does a theoretical term acquire meaning?' he replies:

Everyone agrees that it derives its meaning from the context of the theory. 'Gene' derives its meaning from genetic theory. 'Electron' is interpreted by the postulates of particle physics. (Carnap [1966], p. 248)

At this point, we are faced with a vicious circle: in order to understand a theoretical term, it is necessary to understand the theory to which it belongs, and to understand the theory it is necessary to understand its theoretical terms. But how then can one 'break into' the theory?

2. From Rational to Genetic Reconstruction of Concepts

A simple answer to the question put at the end of the preceding paragraph comes immediately to mind: we acquire the meaning of the theoretical terms

---

[1] Every x is such that if it is placed in water then it dissolves if and only if it is soluble.

of a theory by *being taught* the theory. Oppenheimer took this line when he wrote:

> The laws of physics... cannot be formulated in terms that can be adequately defined without a long period of education, and this is true also of other subjects... We cannot talk about the actual discoveries of biology in everyday terms. We cannot talk about them by referring only to facts of common experience. (Oppenheimer [1962], pp. 108, 112)

Quine shares Oppenheimer's opinion on this subject but he pushed the matter much further and raised this common-sense view to the level of a philosophical thesis:

> ... the scientist himself can make no sense of the language of scientific theory beyond what goes into his learning of it. The paths of language learning, which lead from observation sentences to theoretical sentences, are the only connection there is between observation and theory. (Quine [1975a], p. 79)

The study of learning has traditionally been assigned to psychologists. As the rational reconstruction of scientific concepts à la Carnap is replaced by a genetic account of them, the epistemologist will be well advised to consult the psychologist:

> ... a conspicuous difference between old epistemology and the epistemological enterprise in this new psychological setting is that we can now make free use of empirical psychology. (Quine [1969], p. 83)

Can we describe Quine as abandoning the conceptual part of traditional foundationalist epistemology to experimental psychology? No. Such a description would be an oversimplification. Whereas Carnap was aiming at *reducing* – first completely, and then partially – theoretical terms to observational terms, Quine tries to *understand* the steps by which we move from observation to scientific theory. "Our objective" Quine says "is still philosophical" (Quine, [1975a], p. 78). One of the objectives left to the philosopher is to provide "a better understanding of the relations between evidence and scientific theory". This elucidation is seen by Quine as a decisive step toward "the formulation of relevant questions to be posed to the experimental psychologist". (Quine [1975a], p. 78)

Speculative reconstruction of learning is allowed not only as a *preliminary* phase – as a way of devising hypotheses about actual learning –

but also as a method for answering questions which fall outside empirical psychology altogether. Quine is interested, for instance, not only in the ways in which the child masters the apparatus of reference but also in the ways in which he *might* have mastered it. To Th. Richards who points out that his account of the learning of objectual quantification fails (Richards [1979], pp. 421–429), Quine replies that he "was not interested in how people learn our actual quantifiers" (Quine [1979a], p. 429). But if this is so, what is the *point* of this *Philosophie des als Ob* – to use Vaihinger's title? Here again the contrast between Carnap and Quine can be illuminating. Carnap tried – unsuccessfully – to bridge the gap between the observational basis and the theory itself, first by definitions and then by reduction sentences. Quine settles for a less ambitious goal: he gives up trying to shorten the immense distance which separates scientific theories from their observational basis but at the same time aims at dividing up this long distance into small segments each of which can be covered by "short leaps of analogy". (Quine [1975a], p. 78)

The leaps need not be the *actual* ones we make. The derivation may be *artificial* and yet achieve its purpose. It is *illuminating* to see that the absolute quantification

(2) '$(\forall x) Fx$'

could have been derived as an abbreviation of

(3) '$(\forall x) (\sim Fx \supset Fx)$',

(4) 'For all x if non Fx then Fx',

which could in turn have been derived from the universal categorical construction

(5) Every α is a β,

by substituting 'thing x such that non Fx' for α and 'thing x such that Fx' for β, even if it has not, in fact, been generated in this way.

3. An Alternative to Doctrinal Foundationalism

The *doctrinal* side of the foundationalist programme is even less realistic than the *conceptual* side: "The hopelessness of grounding natural science upon immediate experience in a firmly logical way was acknowledged [by Hume]" (Quine [1969], p. 74). If this is so, what is left for the epistemologist to do? Quine offers him a new field: the empirical study of the human subject in interaction with his environment, i.e. the empirical study of

> The relation between the meager input accorded to human subjects [certain patterns of stimulation of their sensory surfaces] and the torrential output [the various scientific theories] that they construct to account for the latter. (Quine [1969], p. 83)

Conceived in this way, "epistemology... simply falls into place as a chapter of psychology and hence of natural science" (Quine [1969], p. 82). Quine coined the label 'Epistemology naturalized' for this new philosophical field.

Traditional epistemology is normative to the extent that it aims at *justifying* the whole of natural sciences by *deducing* it from its observational basis. With this goal in sight, the traditional epistemologist would be ill advised to draw upon the findings of natural science. If he did so he would be accused of committing a *petitio principii*.

On the contrary, naturalized epistemology aims at *describing* and *explaining* the relations between scientific theories and their observation basis. This shift of goals has methodological consequences of major importance. The threat of circularity vanishes. As Quine notes:

> If we are out simply to understand the link between observation and science, we are well advised to use any available information, including that provided by the very science whose link with observation we are seeking to understand. (Quine [1969], p. 76)

Take, for example, the problem of explaining the success of induction. It is a fact that induction succeeds. Now induction itself rests on *similarity standards* which are subjective. "We predict in the light of observed uniformities, and these are uniformities by our subjective similarity standards" (Quine [1975a], p. 70). If induction succeeds, it is because our subjective similarity standards match up with objective similarities to a certain extent. Why is this so? The theory of natural selection provides an answer: "Creatures inveterately wrong in their inductions have a pathetic but praiseworthy tendency to die before reproducing their kind." (Quine [1969], p. 126)

Here again if Quine's aim had been the traditional one, i.e. to *justify* induction, his recourse to Darwin's theory, which itself is supposed to rest on induction, would have exposed him to the charge of circularity. But when Quine set as his goal the task of *explicating* knowledge, rather than that of laying its foundations, he became immune to this objection:

> I am not appealing to Darwinian biology to justify induction. This would be circular, since biological knowledge depends on induction. Rather I am granting the efficacy of induction, and then observing that Darwinian biology, if true, helps explain why induction is as efficacious as it is. (Quine [1975a], p. 70)

4. The Scope and the Limits of Epistemology Naturalized[1]

If this was all Quine had to say about epistemology naturalized, one might complain that he has opened up a new field of inquiry (naturalized epistemology) rather than contributed to traditional epistemology understood as the task of answering the sceptics who cast doubt on knowledge in general.

Quine tackles this problem in *The Roots of Reference* where he brings naturalized epistemology to bear on the traditional problem of *validating* or *substantiating* our claims to knowledge of the external world. Traditional epistemologists tried to validate our belief in the *external* world by deducing it from our sense data. They refrained from appealing to any *physical fact* or *scientific data* at this stage to avoid circularity. Quine argues that their fear is unjustified:

> This fear of circularity is a case of needless logical timidity, even granted the project of substantiating our knowledge of the external world. The crucial logical point is that the epistemologist is confronting a challenge to natural science that arises from within natural science. (Quine [1974], p. 2)

For instance the question 'How can we derive the existence of a three-dimensional world out of two-dimensional sense-data?' is not as we might think a question which pressupposes a naïve *phenomenological* standpoint.

---
[1] On this topic see Clavelin [1983].

The question arises also within *physical* science since visual sense-data were described as two-dimensional "for no other reason than the physical fact that the surface of the eye is two-dimensional" (Quine [1974], p. 2). One could rephrase Quine's position in these terms: the traditional epistemologist has been mistakenly described as trying to answer a *philosophical* question about the reliability of science as a whole from a standpoint outside science when he was, in fact, trying to dissipate a sceptical doubt which is a 'scientific' doubt.

5. Immanent Versus Transcendent Epistemology

In his reply to Stroud's essay on the "Significance of Naturalized Epistemology" (Quine [1981 b], p. 474), Quine made the following three statements:

(a) What ... does our overall scientific theory really claim regarding the world? Only that it is somehow so structured as to assure the sequences of stimulation that our theory gives us to expect. More concrete demands are indifferent to our scientific theory itself, what with the freedom of proxy functions.

(b) Yet people, sticks, stones, electrons, and molecules are real indeed, on my view, and it is these and no dim proxies that science is all about.

(c) [It] ... is within science itself, and not in some prior philosophy, that reality is properly to be identified and described.

Recently, Sosa objected that (a), (b), and (c) "form an incoherent triad" (Sosa [1983], p. 69), on the ground that

... if we think there really are sticks and stones, then we can't have science accept only a world "somehow so structured as to assure" certain sequences of stimulations or the like. Our science must also claim that there really are sticks and stones. (Sosa [1983], p. 69)

Sosa's objection, however, can be disposed of if we locate statements (a), (b) and (c) at different levels, i.e., (a) and (c) at the level of *metatheory* (a description of building theory) and (b) at the level of *theory*. Quine himself made a move of this kind in his reply to J.C. Smart. The latter anticipated Sosa's objections to Quine by contrasting the 'pragmatism and instrumentalism' of *From a Logical Point of View* with the dominant realism of *Word and Object*. Quine, however, contended that he had not changed his mind and quoted a passage in *Word and Object* in which he allocates his alleged pragmatism and his acknowledged realism to different levels.

> Everything to which we concede existence is a posit from the standpoint of a description of the theory-building process and simultaneously real from the standpoint of the theory that is being built. (Quine quoted in Quine [1968a], p. 265)

However, even if the charge of inconsistency is dismissed, statement (c) remains open to another sort of objection. One can criticize it for being dogmatic and unmotivated.

In several places, Quine expresses agreement with Neurath who "has likened science to a boat which, if we are to rebuild it, we must rebuild plank by plank while staying afloat in it" (Quine [1960a], p. 3). Whoever subscribes to the philosophical standpoint expressed by such a metaphor will say as Quine does, that "the philosopher and the scientist are in the same boat" (Quine [1960a], p. 3), and will deny the philosopher the possibility of rebuilding science as workmen rebuild boats in a dry dock.

The view that there is no first philosophy and that it is up to the scientist to decide what is real, is one which follows from Neurath's metaphor, but it would be naïve to use the metaphor to support it. The traditional epistemologist would rightly object that the metaphor itself was in need of justification. We need to see what can be said to support either Neurath's metaphor or Quine's naturalism.

For the purpose of clarification let us distinguish between (a) *immanent* questions and (b) *transcendent* questions. The former are raised from within science or common sense, common sense being nothing but science in its infancy. The latter are raised from an external vantage point. With this terminology at our disposal, we can describe the epistemologist who considers as open "the general possibility that the objective world is different from the way we take it to be" (Stroud [1981], p. 468) as raising a transcendent question in our sense of the word.

Quine, however, does not criticize the 'traditional' answer to the transcendent question, he goes further and attacks the *question* itself. From a naturalist standpoint, he says the question disappears:

> What evaporates is the transcendental question of the reality of the external world – the question whether or in how far our science measures up to the *Ding an sich*. (Quine [1981a], p. 22)

This statement has a familiar ring. It reminds us of the logical positivist's dismissal of metaphysical questions as illegitimate. But the claim that questions of a certain sort are illegitimate or meaningless requires a justification. To support a claim of that sort logical positivists used to invoke the verification principle: a question which only admits of an answer which in principle cannot be verified is a pseudo-question. (See, for example, A.J. Ayer in *Language, Truth and Logic*.)

Unfortunately the verification principle is open to a powerful objection: it is not itself verifiable. As Putnam observes

... positivist exclusion principles are always self-referentially inconsistent. In short, *positivism produced a conception of rationality so narrow as to exclude the very activity of producing that conception.* (Putnam [1982], p. 18)

To rescue the principle from self-refutation, its proponents gave it the status of a *proposal*. But such a reply is not convincing. The traditional epistemologist is free to turn it down: a proposal is like a piece of advice. It can be ignored.

Moreover, if we scrutinize the role of this proposal we see that in fact it is nothing more than a *hidden metaphysical statement*. This point has been well established by J. Ruytinx:

The logical procedure of 'linguistic proposal' does not seem to confer to the [positivist] doctrine the power of identifying metaphysical expressions without becoming itself metaphysical for that procedure is correlated with the singling out, within a set of rules of language, of a series of privileged statements belonging to the Empiricist doctrine ... The statements thus isolated, however, are not arbitrarily singled out. Their selection is done on purpose: i.e., as a way of withdrawing them from the set of metaphysical expressions. (Ruytinx [1962], p. 225)

Quine repeatedly took an anti-transcendentalist stance on the metaphysical problem of the reality of the external world, but with interesting variations. In 1954, he takes as meaningless not the *question* of the reality of the external world, but the sceptic's answer to it. The following passage by Quine could have been written by a follower of the later Wittgenstein. It sounds like an application of the *paradigm case argument*, rather than an application of the verification principle:

We cannot significantly question the reality of the external world, or deny that there is evidence of external objects in the testimony of our senses; for, to do so is simply to dissociate the terms 'reality' and 'evidence' from the very applications which originally did most to invest those terms with whatever intelligibility they may have for us. (Quine [1954], p. 229)

In the following passage (1960), however, Quine implicitly describes as *meaningless* transcendental claims about the truth or the adequacy of our theories considered *from without:*

Unless pretty firmly and directly conditioned to sensory stimulation, a sentence S is meaningless except relative to its own theory; meaningless intertheoretically.
  Where it makes sense to apply 'true' is to a sentence couched in the terms of a given theory and seen from within the theory ... (Quine [1960a], p. 24)

Although no appeal is made to the verification principle, the dismissal of transcendent questions is clearly a consequence of the adoption of an empiricist theory of meaningfulness.

Finally there is the recent statement (1982) quoted above where Quine describes the transcendental question as 'evaporating'. This claim clearly has a positivist ring to it, and we shall have to examine the arguments put forward to back it up. Such examination will reveal, I contend, that Quine has a new argument to support the rejection of transcendental questions, an argument which is independent of the verification principle.

6. Ontological Relativity and Transcendental Questions

To back up his dismissal of transcendent(al) questions, Quine has recently brought the relativity of ontology to bear on the issue. Addressing himself to Stroud's question, i.e., the question of whether the world could be completely different in general from the way our sensory impacts and our internal makeup lead us to think of it (Stroud [1981], p. 468), he suggests that we "view this possibility in the perspective of proxy functions and displaced ontologies" (Quine [1981b], p. 473). The adoption of such a perspective reveals "that displacements of our ontology" – i.e. our domains of reference – through proxy functions *preserve* the scientific system conceived of as a "conceptual bridge of our own making, linking sensory stimulations to sensory stimulation". (Quine [1981a], p. 20)

If distinct ontologies can be grafted onto scientific systems which are empirically equivalent, i.e., if "it is possible ... to find that there are several referentially distinct yet equivalent sets of correspondence relations which characterize [our] own case, ..." we are, as Hauptli rightly emphasizes "unable to make a legitimate choice amongst this variety ..." (Hauptli [1983], p. 24). Hence, the traditional epistemologist who raises a question requiring a choice of this sort raises an *illegitimate question*. The meaninglessness of the latter is an immediate consequence of the relativity of ontology, which, as we have seen, can be supported by independent arguments. Hence the meaninglessness of transcendent questions can be established without having recourse to controversial principles such as the verification principle. This result is a major achievement of the *Positivismus Streit*.

7. The Immanence of Truth and the Disappearance of Transcendent Questions

In *Theories and Things*, Quine uses the notion of 'immanence' to mitigate the devastating effects of the relativity of ontology. He develops Neurath's metaphor of the philosopher seen as a sailor who repairs his boat at sea:

Staying aboard our own language and not rocking the boat, we are borne smoothly along on it and all is well; 'rabbit' denotes rabbits, and there is no sense in asking 'Rabbits in what sense of "rabbit"?' Reference goes inscrutable if, rocking the boat, we contemplate a permutational mapping of our language on itself, or if we undertake translation. (Quine [1981a], p. 20)

On the next page Quine makes the following comment on the *epistemological* significance of two of his theses: the inscrutability of reference and the relativity of ontology

But it is a confusion to suppose that we can stand aloof and recognize all the alternative ontologies as true in their several ways, all the envisaged worlds as real.
... Truth is immanent, and there is no higher. We must speak from within a theory, albeit any of various. (Quine [1981a], p. 21–22)

The picture of the boat which we are rocking while staying on it is illuminating. It supersedes the classical picture of the transcendental philosopher trying to describe the limits of knowledge. This classical picture raises a difficulty which Wittgenstein has seen but not solved: to think a limit one has to think of both of its sides. But when one tries to conceive the limits of meaningfulness on this model, a paradox results since the picture suggests that the transcendental epistemologist is able to think the unthinkable, or to say the unsayable.

... we cannot say, there is this and this in the world, but not that, for to say so would apparently presuppose that we exclude certain possibilities, and this cannot be the case, since it would require that logic should go beyond the boundaries of the world as if it could contemplate these boundaries from the other side also. What we cannot think we cannot think, therefore we also cannot say what we cannot think. (Wittgenstein [1922] preface by Russell p. XVIII)

Quine's development of Neurath's metaphor of the boat repaired at sea avoids that paradox. Not only can we repair the boat while staying on it, but we can also rock the boat. Contemplating a permutational mapping of our language on itself replaces the impossible task of contemplating the boundaries from the other side. It teaches us this lesson of epistemology: isomorphic ontologies seen from without are equivalent.

On this view, ontology is still legitimate, but, so to speak, immanent as opposed to transcendent; i.e., general ontological questions are legitimate only when raised *from within* the 'web' or the 'field of force' of our scientific beliefs. Ontology can be salvaged by becoming a part of science. Thus, transcendent questions become respectable only when they become immanent.

Transcendent questions for Quine are, I contend, nothing but a hangover of traditional metaphysics from which we should free ourselves. Ideally, transcendent questions should disappear completely, they should be swallowed by immanent ones in the same way as the interior-exterior contrast disappears in a Moebius strip where there is only one surface left, as we can see if we try to paint it. Quine could be described as a philosopher who starts with the transcendent-immanent opposition, but supersedes it and operates a sort of hegelian *Aufhebung*: in the end transcendental questions evaporate altogether and immanent ontology occupies the ground. To put it briefly, ontology *seen from without* is relative. *Seen from within* it is *not*.

8. Difficulties Arising from the Conception of Truth as Immanent to Theories

If truth is immanent to theories, it can no longer be used as a yardstick to assess and evaluate theories. But this is not a serious loss. As Davidson rightly observed

> The trouble is that the notion of fitting the totality of experience, like the notion of fitting the facts, or being true to the facts, adds nothing intelligible to the simple concept of being true ...
> Nothing, however, no *thing*, makes sentences and theories true: not experience, not surface irritations, not the world. (D. Davidson [1973], p. 16)[1]

But this does not mean that agreement with empirical evidence ceases to play the role of a *norm* in the evaluation of our theories. The role of experience is displaced but not abandoned. Quine brought that out in his reply to Davidson:

> The proper role of experience ... is as a basis not for truth but for warranted belief ... Empiricism as a theory of truth ... goes by the board ... As a theory of evidence, however, empiricism remains with us, minus indeed the two old dogmas. (Quine [1981a], p. 39)

To put it in a nutshell, although truth is immanent to theories, there is a crowbar which is *transcendent* to *theories*: *empirical evidence*. Hence there are more normative components in Quine's epistemology than meets the eye.

Putnam complains that truth defined à la Tarski, as a disquotation device "cannot serve as the primitive notion of epistemology or of methodology" (Putnam, [1982], p. 19). He argues as follows: if we expel the notion of *justification* from epistemology as too inaccessible an ideal, and, if we introduce instead the normative notion of reliability, we shall be committed to define a "reliable method not as a method which yields *true* results", but, a "method which yields verdicts *I* accept" (Putnam [1982], p. 20) and this, he says, commits us "to a solipsism of the present moment". Admittedly one could try to meet the objection by bringing in the concept of "a verdict I would accept *in the long run*", but this way out, "would at once involve one with the use of counterfactuals", and with such notions as "similarity of possible worlds". (Putnam [1982], p. 21)

---

[1] See, however, Mulligan, Simons, Smith, [1984].

Putnam is right when he says that for Quine,

truth, as defined by Tarski is not a *property* of statements at all, but a syncategorematic notion which enables us to "ascend semantically", i.e. to talk about sentences instead of about objects. (Putnam [1982], p. 19)

But he is wrong, in our opinion, to conclude that the adoption of a concept of truth which states that 'to call a statement true is just to reaffirm it' entails the dismissal of a *normative* epistemology. As I have pointed out above the 'tribunal of experience' retains its role whatever account of the predicate 'true' we favour.

There is, however, a last difficulty to consider. Quine has put forward the claim that there could be conflicting theories which are empirically equivalent. This thesis called 'the underdetermination of scientific theories by observational data', from now on TUD, will be expounded shortly. At this point I will limit myself to formulating the following problem: if TUD is combined with the claim that truth is immanent to theories, we are forced to admit several conflicting truths, hence relativism threatens Quine after all.

Notice that the sort of relativism which results is a very special one. It does not make the notion of scientific progress *inapplicable*. Progress consisting of the rejection of disconfirmed theories can still exist. We observe an interesting asymmetry: we can escape from what is false – by getting rid of disconfirmed theories – but not approximate to what is true, since there may be rival theories which have an equal right to count as true.

9. The Originality of TUD

TUD was formulated for the first time in *Word and Object*. One of the neatest and shortest formulations goes back to a paper of 1970:

... many people will agree ... that physical theory is underdetermined even by all *possible* observations ... Theory can still vary though all possible observations be fixed. Physical theories can be at odds with each other and yet compatible with all possible data even in the broadest sense. In a word, they can be logically incompatible and empirically equivalent. (Quine [1970b], p. 179)

Quine's TUD has had forerunners.[1] H. Weyl writes in his *Philosophy of Mathematics and Science* (1949):

The possibility must not be rejected that several different constructions might be suitable to explain our perceptions; in this recognition of the 'ambiguity of truth', Hobbes and D'Alembert preceded the modern positivists. (Weyl [1949], p. 153)

Weyl, however, speaks of 'perceptions'. Moreover, he does not specify whether he has in mind *'actual* perceptions', i.e., *past, present and future perceptions*, or whether he means a larger set, namely 'actual plus possible perceptions'. Yet the difference is of considerable importance. If the narrower interpretation is given (perceptions = actual perceptions), then we can say that Hobbes and d'Alembert anticipated the Duhem-Quine thesis. If, however, 'perceptions' is given the wider interpretation, then they anticipated TUD. It is probably safe to say that they anticipated neither, although they conceived a doctrine which, when made precise, can lead to the Duhem-Quine thesis or to TUD.

The main argument which Quine offers in support of TUD runs as follows:

Scientists invent hypotheses that talk of things beyond the reach of observation. The hypotheses are related to observation only by a kind of one-way implication; namely, the events we observe are what a belief in the hypotheses would have led us to expect. These observable consequences of the hypotheses do not, conversely, imply the hypotheses. Surely there are alternative hypothetical substructures that would surface in the same observable ways. (Quine [1975b], p. 313)

Commenting on this argument, Bergström writes:

This seems plausible enough, but it remains to be shown that such 'alternative hypothetical substructures' may be logically incompatible. (L. Bergström [1984], p. 352)

Bergström's observation is important. Quine's main argument fails to establish his own version of TUD. It only supports a *weaker* claim which can be described as the disjunction of two distinct versions of TUD, i.e., that which states that the alternative hypothetical substructures are *logically incompatible* and that which states that the alternative hypothetical substructures are simply *different*, i.e., are such that *neither entails the other*.

---

[1] I owe this to Johan van Benthem.

Let us now examine another notion which occurs in the formulation of TUD, the notion of 'empirical equivalence'. In the 1970 formulation, Quine uses the expression 'empirically equivalent theories' but not until 1975 did he give a technical definition of this crucial notion. Before we state it, we need to define two preliminary notions, the notion of a *pegged observation sentence* and the notion of an *observational conditional*.

A theory T fits the set of observations $\{O_1 \ldots O_n\}$ if T logically implies the observation-sentence $OS_1 \ldots OS_n$. But observation sentences are occasion sentences, i.e. *tensed* sentences. As the classical relation of entailment is defined for standing sentences, observation sentences should be replaced by what Quine calls *pegged observation sentences*, i.e., observation sentences in which the verb is tenseless but which incorporate a place-time specification or, better still, they should be replaced by *observational conditionals*, i.e., conditionals whose antecedent expresses boundary conditions, and whose consequent is a pegged observation sentence. Notice, however, that "The time and place may be beyond the reach of all sentient life" (Quine [1975b], p. 317). One could also define possible observations *directly*, instead of defining them through the definition of observation sentences, in this way:

... a *possible observation* of S according to [theory] T is the meter reading that T says would result if an initially noninteracting system S' were allowed to interact with S in a prescribed manner. (Wilson [1980], p. 220)

The definition of the *set of possible* observations follows directly:

The *set of possible observations* permitted by T is the collection of quadruples $\langle S, S', r, t\rangle$ where S and S' are possible systems of T and r is the meter reading (if any) that obtains as S' interacts with S at t. (Wilson [1980], p. 220)

The definition of the empirical equivalence of theories can be given readily. Two theories are *empirically equivalent* if they logically imply the same set of observation conditionals (such as, for example, 'If the wind is blowing at 41° N and 70° W on March 9, 1981, at 05.00 then it's raining at 42° N and 71° W on March 10, 1981 at 02.00').

It is not difficult to find theories which are both empirically equivalent and logically incompatible, but very often the logical incompatibility can be explained away by a *reconstrual* of *predicates*. When this is the case, the two theories are *mere* notational variants of each other. Quine himself gives the following example of two theories which are only 'pseudo'-competitors.

Take some theory formulation and select two of its terms, say 'electron' and 'molecule'. I am supposing that these do not figure essentially in any observation sentences; they are purely theoretical. Now let us transform our theory formulation merely by switching these two terms throughout. The new theory formulation will be logically incompatible with the old: it will affirm things about so-called electrons that the other denies. Yet their only difference, the man in the street would say, is terminological; the one theory formulation uses the technical terms 'molecule' and 'electron' to name what the other formulation calls 'electron' and 'molecule'. The two formulations express, he would say, the same theory. (Quine, [1975b], p. 319)

Quine also refuses to count as genuinely, and not merely verbally different, the two cosmologies described by Poincaré, one of which represents space as infinite whilst the other represents it as finite, but depicts all objects as shrinking in proportion as they move away from the centre. The reason why he rejects this example is that it is possible in this case, as it is in the first, to make the two theories coincide verbally by means of a reconstrual of predicates. (Quine [1979], p. 67)

Newton-Smith, has spelt out two purported exemplifications of TUD. In the first example, he considers two theories 'Time is linear and history is precisely cyclical (T_1)' and 'Time is closed (T_2)'. Quine dismissed this example as he dissmissed Poincaré's example and for the same reason.

Newton-Smith's second illustration concerns Newton's mechanics (T_3) and Notwen's mechanics (T_4). The latter is a version of the former in which the postulate that space and time are continuous has been replaced by the postulate that space and time are merely dense and not continuous.

Quine did not react to Newton-Smith's second example. Yet it is an interesting one. One cannot dismiss it by saying that T_3 and T_4 are pseudo-competitors which can be made to coincide verbally by means of a reconstrual of predicates. It is well known that there is no mapping of the set of rational numbers onto the set of real numbers, hence no mapping of T_4's space and time onto T_3's space and time. Newton-Smith's second example, however, can be criticized on other grounds. L. Bergström argues that the point on which T_3 and T_4 diverge is a gratuitous extension:

... it seems to me that since the two conflicting postulates "space and time are continuous" and "space and time are dense" affect neither the empirical content nor the explanatory power of the two theories, they can just as well be removed, leaving, as it were, the core of Newtonian mechanics. (This core might be stated as the disjunction of what Newton-Smith regards as Newton's mechanics and Notwen's mechanics.) (L. Bergström [1984], pp. 351–52)

To exclude these unsatisfactory examples of TUD, Bergström refined the notion of underdetermination by introducing the notion of *strict underdetermination*.

First, let us say that a theory is *tight* if it is not a gratuitous extension of any theory. We may then say that a theory is *strictly underdetermined* if and only if it is tight and logically incompatible with some empirically equivalent tight theory. (L. Bergström [1984], p. 351)

This is clearly faithful to Quine's intention since Quine explicitly restricts the predicate 'underdetermined' to theories which exhibit *unavoidable branching* as opposed to *possible branching*.

In order to avoid the trivialization of TUD which would result if pseudo-competitors were not excluded, Quine offers a criterion for the individuation of theories which takes reconstrual of predicates into account: Two empirically equivalent theories are really, and not only verbally, different when there exists no reconstrual of predicates 'however devious', which makes them logically equivalent to each other. By *reconstrual* of predicates, Quine means "any mapping of our lexicon of predicates into our open sentences (n-place predicates to n-variable sentences)". (Quine [1975b], p. 320)

Though the reconstrual of predicates can be devious, it should be subject, I think, to certain systematic constraints. If it were not subject to any constraints, it would always be possible to find a mapping which would make two initially competing theories coincide, and TUD would simply become trivially false. What are these constraints like? Quine gives us a hint in "The Nature of Natural Knowledge" where he speaks of *rules* of *translation*:

Where the significant difference comes is perhaps where we no longer see how to state rules of translation that would bring the two empirically equivalent theories together. (Quine [1975a], p. 80–81)

A clear case of *rule-governed* translation is provided by the way we switch back and forth from decimal to binary notation. As a minimal constraint we might, therefore, require the existence of a *function* which maps the sentences of theory T onto those of theory T' and insist that the function be computable.

10. The Threat of Relativism Generated by TUD

We said that if we combine TUD with the claim that truth is immanent to theories, relativism ensues. This danger did not escape Quine's notice. In "Empirically Equivalent Systems of the World" he comes to grips with the problem:

> Perhaps there are two best theories that imply all the true observation conditionals and no false ones. The two are equally simple, let us suppose, and logically incompatible ...
> Can we say that one, perhaps, is true, and the other therefore false, but that it is impossible in principle to know which? (Quine [1975b], p. 327)

First, he tried to ward off the objection by using the manoeuvre he has recourse to in the context of ontological relativity: he appeals to conservatism

> ... there is no extra-theoretic truth, no higher truth than the truth we are claiming or aspiring to as we continue to tinker with our system of the world from within. If ours were one of those two rival best theories that we imagined a moment ago, it would be our place to insist on the truth of our laws and the falsity of the other theory where it conflicts. (Quine [1975b], p. 327)

Quine, however, is aware that when we say that *our* theory is preferable, as far as truth is concerned, to the rival theory, we *rise* above our own theory and in this respect make a *transcendent* and *intertheoretic* use of the predicate 'true', hence an *illegitimate* use by his own standards. Remember that Quine wrote in *Word and Object*: "Unless pretty firmly and directly conditioned to sensory stimulation, a sentence S is meaningless except relative to its own theory, meaningless intertheoretically." (Quine [1960a], p. 24).

This is the *paradox of cultural relativism*:

> He [the cultural relativist] cannot proclaim cultural relativism without rising above it, and he cannot rise above it without giving it up. (Quine [1975b], p. 328)

Quine, however, boldly chose to rise above cultural relativism[1]:

---

[1] TUD combined with naturalized epistemology also leads to a kind of Relativism as Martha Feher has recently observed (Feher, [forthcoming]): "if epistemology is regarded ... as ... part of ... empirical psychology, then it becomes subjected to the underdetermination thesis ...". Quine would agree with this. He recognizes the possibility that "... another culture ... guided by norms that differ sharply from ours ... (might) predict as successfully ... as we". (Quine [1981a], p. 181)

It is the extreme situation where we would do well to settle for a frank dualism. Oscillation between rival theories is standard scientific procedure anyway, for it is thus that one explores and assesses alternative hypotheses. Where there is forever no basis for choosing, then, we may simply rest with both systems and discourse freely in both, using distinctive signs to indicate which game we are playing. (Quine [1975b], p. 328)

Here, however, Newton-Smith contends that Relativism leads to silence.

It is no comfort to learn that to proclaim that doctrine lands us in paradox. At best that would leave us in a *Tractatus* silence. If Quine is right we have been shown that there is truth in cultural relativism even though (because of that paradox) we cannot say that there is truth there. (Newton-Smith [1981], p. 181–182)

One could, however, resist Newton-Smith's claim and conceive of a third theory from which we could *describe* the two conflicting theories without having any means to *rank* them. If so, Quine would not be reduced to silence.[1]

Newton-Smith in ([1978] pp. 87, 88) had formulated a serious, but less important, objection against Quine with the following dilemma. Let us assume that one has sympathy with a realist position and that one has adopted a 'correspondence' theory of truth, in the sense that a proposition is true or false in virtue of how the world is. Let us also assume that one believes in the Law of Bivalence which claims that any proposition is either true or false. The realist who is confronted with TUD can adopt two attitudes. The first response, which Newton-Smith calls the *ignorance response* involves supposing that there are inaccessible facts, facts concerning which we have no evidence. The second response, which Newton-Smith calls the *arrogance response*, involves restricting realism in the following sense: 'given a context in which some proposition P is empirically undecidable, the assumption that either P is true or P is false is withdrawn'.

What is Quine's response to that dilemma? Quine seems to oscillate between the ignorance and the arrogance response. In his reply to Chomsky, he draws a sharp contrast between indeterminacy of translation and TUD. This contrast is relevant for the present discussion since inscrutability of reference and ontological relativity go hand in hand with the indeterminacy of translation:

---

[1] I owe this point to Frank Veltman.

> ... where indeterminacy of translation applies, there is no real question of right choice; there is no fact of the matter even to *within* the acknowledged under-determination of a theory of nature. (Quine, [1968b], p. 275)

This seems to suggest that as far as TUD is concerned, there is, *a contrario*, a fact of the matter and a right choice.

In *Theories and Things*, however, Quine seems to favour the arrogance response and to adopt an instrumentalist view of the role of theories:

> Our scientific theory can indeed go wrong, and precisely in the familiar way: through failure of predicted observation. But what if, happily and unbeknownst, we have achieved a theory that is conformable to every possible observation, past and future? In what sense could the world then be said to deviate from what the theory claims? Clearly in none, even if we can somehow make sense of the phrase 'every possible observation'. Our overall scientific theory demands of the world only that it be so structured as to assure the sequences of stimulation that our theory gives us to expect. More concrete demands are empty, what with the freedom of proxy functions. (Quine [1981a], p. 22)

This instrumentalist interpretation of theories is already present in the 1975 paper ("On Empirically Equivalent Systems of the World") where TUD is characterized as follows:

> Here, evidently, is the nature of under-determination. There is some infinite lot of observation conditionals that we want to capture in a finite formulation.
> ... Any finite formulation that will imply them is going to have to imply also some trumped-up matter, or stuffing, whose only service is to round out the formulation. There is some freedom of choice of stuffing, and such is the under-determination. (Quine [1975b], p. 324)

In other words, were it not the case that a Craigian elimination of theoretical terms fails to comply with the requirements of a finitist formulation, Quine would favour a formulation in which theoretical terms have been eliminated completely. It is implicit in that passage that TUD has no bite when theories are given a Craigian formulation.

A realist might object that, once we have decided to comply with the finitist constraint, we are entitled to say that one of the two finite rival formulations might be more in accordance with how the world is than the other, even if we are not able to tell which. At this stage one could defend Quine's position by dismissing the correspondence theory of truth which lies behind the realist's worry as a relic of the transcendent theory of truth which Quine has abandoned. Such a defence amounts to adopting the arrogance response and to making TUD less important and disquieting than it seemed to be at first sight.

Quine's own reply in the passage of *Theories and Things* quoted p. 121 is not satisfactory in my opinion: it explains why there is no fact of the matter behind rival theories which differ by their ontologies but it does not come to grips with another sort of conflict, i.e. the conflict which exists between two theories which share the same ontology but which ascribe incompatible predicates to the same entities.

A more radical answer to this problem can be found in *Theories and Things*. It amounts to reconciling the apparently rival theories. This solution will be examined now.

Let θ_1 and θ_2 be two theories which are logically incompatible, but empirically equivalent. Since they are empirically equivalent, both θ_1 and θ_2 imply the same set of observation conditionals, i.e., $\{\varphi_1 \supset \psi_1, \ldots, \varphi_n \supset \psi_n\}$. And since, by assumption, the two theories are *incompatible*, "... the two theory formulations that we are imagining must evaluate some sentence [occurring in both] oppositely" (Quine [1981a], p. 29). In other words there must be a theoretical sentence p_i which is asserted by one of the theories, and whose negation $\sim p_i$ is asserted by the other. For example, it might be that θ_1 asserts 'Neutrinos have a mass', whilst θ_2 asserts 'Neutrinos do not have a mass'.

The solution which Quine recommends in his latest book is to eliminate the contradiction between the two sentences by treating certain short words occurring in both of them as if they were distinct terms:

... we can just as well pick out one of those terms and treat it as if it were two independent words, one in the one theory formulation and another in the other. We can mark this by changing the spelling of the word in one of the two theory formulations. (Quine [1981a], pp. 29–30)

Thus in our example one would preserve 'neutrinos' in the first sentence, but write 'newtrinos', for instance, in the second. The result is that by "pressing this trivial expedient, we can resolve all conflicts between the two theory formulations. Both can be admitted thenceforward as true descriptions of one and the same world in different terms" (Quine, [1981a], p. 30). The theories are still *different*, but as they are now compatible they can both be adopted at the same time. One is no longer forced to oscillate.

This solution amounts to transforming a case of *strict* underdetermination (*logical incompatibility* of theories which share the same empirical content) into a case of *strong* incompatibility (*logical independance* of theories sharing the same empirical content), to borrow Bergström's terminology. The trouble is that the conjunction of two logically independant theories into a single theory leads to a very weak theory. The resulting theory is weak because all the ontological commitments which are made by one of the theories alone have to be dropped by a non-controversial application of Ockham's razor. The point is made by Bergström in the following terms:

Suppose, e.g. that one and only one of the theories postulates the existence of electrons ... For, as the theory is ... underdetermined, all the evidence can be accounted for by other theories, which do not entail the assumption that there are electrons. Hence, we have no genuine support for this assumption. (Bergström [1984], p. 353–354)

Shall we count the two theories reconciled by the trivial expedient mentioned above as *two theories* or as *one tandem theory*? If we take the first line, we are forced to take one of them as the frame of reference for the predicate "true", since truth is immanent to theories, and this choice is arbitrary. If we take the second line, we are forced to violate the maxim of simplicity by implicitly accepting what Feigl called 'epistemological danglers', i.e. empirically empty components.

In "Meaning, Reference and Truth" (forthcoming), Quine recognized the strength of this objection: "A portion of a theory is a dangler if it contributes none to empirical coverage. The theory minus the dangler is equivalent to the theory including the dangler. In combining two rival theories to form a tandem theory, I admitted danglers." (Quine [forthcoming])

He now prefers to take the sectarian line again and to choose one of the two different but irreconcilable theories. To make Quine's "sectarism" more palatable, one should bear in mind that the two theories are logically compatible and that they enjoy the property of warranted assertability. Hence we are not asked to make a blind choice between good and evil, but a blind choice between two equally good theories, for the sake of simplicity. We should not be surprised that Quine accepts to describe the two theories as equally well warranted and refuses to call them true. The predicate "true" makes sense only *within* a theory since truth is *immanent* to theories.

Warranted assertability, on the contrary, has to do with *evidence*, which *transcends* theories.

To eradicate the tendency to make an intertheoretic use of "true" in this context, Quine describes the two rival theories as "incommensurable": "Those as Kuhn, Paul Feyerabend and others allude persistently to incommensurability of theories. The notion has struck me as empty, but in the present context, I seem to make sense of it: the context of two empirically equivalent but irreducible systems of the world." (ibid.)

11. An Assessment of TUD

Quine looks at physics as a logician, not as a physicist. His account of science is too *static*. Since he puts observation terms and theoretical concepts in the same basket, he underrates the role of the rules of correspondence which connect observation terms with theoretical concepts. It would be more *realistic* to see empirical equivalence as *relative* to the set of correspondence rules accepted at a given time. Should a case of empirical equivalence occur, it would be seen as an incentive to search for additional rules of correspondence leading to experiments whose results would enable us to discriminate between the rival theories. The very notion of a complete set of possible observation conditionals does not do justice to the way science evolves[1].

Let us consider Lorentz' physics versus Einstein's relativity theory. Each of these two physical theories accounted for the negative result of the Michelson and Morley experiment. Yet Einstein's theory was adopted. There is a major theoretical difference between the two. In Lorentz' theory, space is absolute, it does not enjoy any physical properties even though it is filled with a physical stuff: Aether. In Einstein's theory, on the contrary, the very concepts of geometry are given a physical interpretation. This is a major theoretical shift. Could Quine's instrumentalist view of theories account for this shift? If we consider the context of justification as opposed to the context of discovery, Quine would account for the choice made by the scientific community in this way: he would appeal to the greater simplicity and elegance of Einstein's theory and also to its increased heuristic value.

---

[1] I owe this point to Th. Kuipers, G. de Vries and J. Oosten.

He would say that although the two theories are on a par with regard to *actual* observations, they are not on a par with respect to the set of *possible* observations. The trouble is that the set of possible observations cannot be defined a priori, once and for all. Changes in the theory lead to changes in the *scope* of the theory and these in turn extend the set of possible observations which are *relevant* to the theory. Quine's static picture of science does not do justice to the relation of mutual dependence which holds between the intended scope or field of application of the theory and the set of possible observations relevant to its confirmation.[1]

The only instances of incompatible theoretical sentences which Quine accepts are sentences the elimination of which would not lead to any change in the set of observational conditionals. It might then be said that the incompatibility is inessential after all.[2]

---

[1] I draw here on a suggestion due to M. Richir.
[2] I owe this to A. Schramm. For a non instrumentalist view of theories, see C. Dilworth, "On Theoretical Words" *Erkenntnis* [1984], pp. 405–421.

V
The Demarcation of Logic

1. Logical Truths and Analyticity

In Chapter I we discussed Quine's critique of the classical definition of analyticity. According to this a statement is analytic if it is either a logical truth, or is reducible to a logical truth by uniform replacement of terms by their synonyms. Thus, since

(1)   All vixens are vixens

is a logical truth and 'vixen' and 'female fox' are synonymous, then

(2)   All vixens are female foxes

is, according to the definition, analytic. We saw, however, that the attempt to explain the analyticity of (2) in this way is in Quine's view circular, since to define synonymity the notion of analyticity itself (or some related notion) is needed.

Plausible though Quine's argument is, it is clear that it cannot be used as an argument against the existence of statements that qualify as analytic on the first count, namely: logical truths. Thus, if the distinction between analytic and synthetic truths cannot be defended in the terms in which it has been stated, it remains an open possibility whether a different distinction can be defended, namely, that between logical truths like (1) and non logical ones like

(3)   Some foxes are silver

And, as we shall see, one of the more illuminating aspects of Quine's work is to have shown that the two distinctions can be treated in radically different ways.

Before trying to substantiate this we must first consider Quine's definition of the notion of logical truth. The key terms in his account are those of an *essential* occurrence and a *vacuous* occurrence, terms which he introduced in an early article "Truth by Convention" (1936). The former of these terms is defined as follows:

A word may be said to occur *essentially* in a statement if replacement of the word by another is capable of turning the statement into a falsehood. (Quine [1940], p. 2)

Thus in the sentence,

(4) Today is Tuesday or it is not Tuesday,

the logical particle 'or' has an essential occurrence; replacement of it by 'if and only if', for example, would result in a falsehood. By contrast 'Tuesday' does not occur essentially; uniform replacement of it by 'Wednesday', for example, merely results in another truth. Because of this its occurrence is what Quine calls a vacuous one:

An expression will be said to occur *vacuously* in a given statement if its replacement therein by any and every other grammatically admissible expression leaves the truth or falsehood of the statement unchanged. (Quine, [1936], p. 80)

Given these explanations, a logical truth may be defined as follows:

... if S'' involves only logical expressions essentially, and hence remains true when everything except that skeleton of logical expressions is changed in all grammatically possible ways, then S'' depends for its truth upon those logical constituents alone, and is thus a truth of logic. (Quine [1936], p. 81)

In his *Philosophy of Logic* Quine expresses this with exemplary lucidity: "... a sentence is logically true if all sentences are true that share its logical structure". (Quine [1970c], p. 49)

Now it seems that this definition not only does not appeal to the notion of synonymity, but does not make use of any other intensional notion either. Hence, the objections to classing (2) as analytic do not seem to apply to the classification of (1) as a logical truth. But is this really so?

It would obviously be difficult to object to the definition for the use it makes of the notion of *truth* itself. Tarski has shown how this notion may be defined for formal languages by using only the resources of extensional semantics. And since Quine argues for a regimentation of natural language into first order predicate calculus, truth can be defined in Tarski's way for natural language so regimented. There is no need to rely, therefore, on Popper's bolder claim that Tarski's theory

> is applicable to any consistent and even to a 'natural' language, if only we learn from Tarski's analysis how to dodge its inconsistencies. (Popper [1963], p. 223)

The other ingredients of the definition of logical truth would seem to be equally inoffensive. One of these is the notion of a vacuous occurrence, which is defined using the *purely syntactical* notion of the substitution of one expression for another. Whilst finally there is a list of logical particles given by enumeration:

> First we suppose indicated, by enumeration if not otherwise, what words are to be called logical words; typical ones are 'or', 'not', 'if', 'then', 'and', 'all', 'every', 'only', 'some'. (Quine [1960b], p. 110)

It is, however, important to note that if the notion of logical truth depends on that of logical particle, and if the logical particles can be given *only* by enumeration, then the extension of the concept of logical truth will be extremely unstable. The contrast between logical and non-logical truths would remain clear-cut, but it would become relatively *arbitrary*. So the issue of what is a logical particle is perhaps the one that raises most of the questions for Quine's definition.

To begin with, Quine was not discomfited by a purely enumerative definition of the concept of logical particle. Interestingly, in his classic paper "On the Concept of Logical Consequence" (1936), Tarski took a similar line, frankly conceding that the boundary between logical and non-logical particles is far from well defined:

> Underlying our whole construction is the division of all terms of the language discussed into logical and extra-logical. This division is certainly not quite arbitrary. If, for example, we were to include among the extra-logical signs the implication sign, or the universal quantifier, then our definition of the concept of consequence would lead to results which obviously contradict ordinary usage. On the other hand, no objective grounds are known to me which permit us to draw a sharp boundary between the two groups of terms. It seems to be possible to include among logical terms some which are usually regarded by logicians as extra-logical without running into consequences which stand in sharp contrast to ordinary language. (Tarski [1956], p. 418)

2. Steps Towards a Definition of the Notion of Logical Particle

But if he was not initially unduly perturbed by a purely enumerative definition of logical particles as envisaged by Tarski, Quine was later to propose a more 'abstract' account of logical truth which seems to avoid the difficulty with his first definition:

> Now the further idea suggests itself of defining logical truth more abstractly, by appealing not specifically to the negation, conjunction, and quantification that figure in our particular object language, but to whatever grammatical constructions one's object language may contain. A logical truth is, on this approach, a sentence whose grammatical structure is such that all sentences with that structure are true. (Quine [1970c], p. 58)

Quine's definition can also be put thus:

> a logical truth is a sentence that cannot be turned false by substituting for lexicon (Quine [1970c], p. 58)

When Quine speaks of lexical substitution, he means a sort of substitution which satisfies *grammatical* requirements. Roughly, the lexical item B which is substituted for A must belong to the same grammatical category as A. But this is not enough. Although 'raining' belongs to the same category as 'pouring', substituting it only for the second occurrence of 'pouring' in 'If it is pouring, it is pouring' does not qualify as a correct substitution. If it did, no truth of logic would remain. From 'If it is pouring it is pouring' we could move to 'If it is pouring, it is raining' and from the latter to 'If it is pouring, it is freezing'. In order to avoid this unwanted consequence, we have to impose an additional constraint upon substitution, i.e. *uniformity*. As A. Dale put it,

> Quine intends his definition to permit only the same substitution for the same lexical unit at all of its occurrences in the sentence.[1]

---

[1] *Added in proof* I owe this to A. Dale who pointed out a mistake of mine and kindly let me read his critical notice forthcoming in the *Revue internationale de Philosophie* 1985 fasc. 4.

The originality of Quine's definitions is unquestionable. In these new definitions the notion of *logical* structure gives way to that of *grammatical* structures; whilst the contrast between *lexicon* and *grammar* replaces the one between logical and non-logical terms. But is anything really gained by these moves?

3. Logical Form and Grammatical Structure

One gain at least is that the latter pair of distinctions is independently motivated. The notion of a grammatical category, together with the associated notion of grammatical structure is indispensable for linguistic theory since the linguist has to describe a potential infinity of sentences by means of a finite formulation. His only hope of succeeding is to analyse the sentences structurally, this enabling him to describe sentences in terms of their constituent categories, presumed finite. For instance, a structure such as predication enables us, by combining a proper name with a predicate, to obtain an atomic sentence, for example, 'John walks'. Thus, one might suggest that a sentence's grammatical structure is the structure it has in terms of the categories needed for the simplest finite formulation of the syntax of the language to which it belongs.

Understood in this way the distinction between grammar and lexicon is not language independent. Hence it is, perhaps, conceivable that it is made in different ways in different languages. But this would not show that Quine's new definition merely shifts the problem. For what is important is that the distinction be clear with respect to a given language, and the fact that it may be drawn differently elsewhere does nothing to suggest that this is not so. And there is good reason to think that a clear distinction can be made in the case of a given language. For there exists a property of grammatical particles that enables one to distinguish them in a clear cut way from lexical items, namely, the fact that they are interchangeable *salva congruitate* – that is without loss of grammaticality – with expressions of a *finite* class. On the other hand, lexical items are interchangeable *salva congruitate* with the expressions of a *potentially infinite* class. For example, in the statement

(5) Either Socrates walks or he does not walk

the particle 'Either ... or ...' can be replaced by 'and', 'because', 'if ... then ...', and 'if and only if', preserving if not *truth*, at least *grammaticality*. The admissible substitutions are the grammatical conjunctions whose number, even if it varies from language to language, nevertheless remains *finite* and relatively *small*. By contrast the lexical item 'Socrates' can be replaced by an *infinitely expandable* number of proper names. As for variables, which are infinite in number, one can rule that they belong *ex officio* to the grammatical part of formal language, a convention which does not endanger the distinction between logical and non-logical terms in natural language, since there are no variables in natural language. The pronouns which play the role of bound variables in natural language (such as 'someone' and 'he' in 'If someone F's he G's') constitute a finite set which raises no problems.

Somebody might object that this still all depends on an arbitrary decision; for what is to stop us treating, for example 'smokes' as a construction, albeit an idiosyncratic one from our current perspective? Might we not then introduce a sign for negation '$\sim$' as a lexical item, so that, as before, we can construct the molecular sentence '$\sim$ (x smokes)' (i.e. 'x does not smoke')? But the difficulty with this alternative is that it makes the task of the linguist impossible. His treatment of the construction *smokes* will be completely *ad hoc* unless he also posits the construction *runs*, the construction *flies*, the construction *dances*, etc. In so doing, however, he ceases to be able to explicate a native speaker's ability to understand a potential infinity of sentences, on the basis of his understanding of a lexicon and a finite number of constructions.

One consequence of Quine's new definition of logical truth is that it enlarges the class of logical truths in intuitively acceptable ways. Consider the following:

(6) Whoever walks rapidly, walks

which, intuitively speaking, is not merely true, but logically so. Restricted to the resources of the lower predicate calculus we would have to symbolize this as being of the form.

(7) $(\forall x)(Fx \supset Gx)$

which is, of course, not a logical truth. This comes about because the symbolism of the lower predicate calculus cannot represent whatever it is that 'walks rapidly' and 'walks' have in common – the 'walks' within 'walks rapidly' is not discernible as it were.

If, as in this case, the structure ascribed by the logician is insufficiently discriminating, it can also be pointlessly fine grained. This would be so, for instance if (8) below was represented by (9a), even though the symbolism of the propositional calculus suffices, as in (9b):

(8)　　If everyone is dancing, then everyone is dancing

(9a)　$(\forall x)\ Fx \supset (\forall x)\ Fx$

(9b)　$p \supset p$

But how can one know that one has represented enough of a statement's structure, but not too much? According to Quine, the maxim that should guide us is that of not exposing more logical structure than the minimum that is *necessary* – adding, as S. Haack urges, *as much* as is necessary – "... it is preferable to think of the optimal formal representation as the one which reveals the least structure consistently with supplying a formal argument which is valid in the system if the informal argument is judged extra-systematically valid". (S. Haack [1978], p. 24)

It is noteworthy that Quine is not committed to postulating a unique logical form for each sentence, since differing levels of structure may be needed to account for the validity of different arguments – for some purposes (9b) would be sufficient, but for others (9a) would be required. His definition also has the merit of throwing new light on the question of possible extensions of logic. There are essentially two ways of extending the domain of logic to encompass wider areas. New lexical categories can be added, or the number of logical constants can be added to. The second of these methods is well known, so let us, to begin with, look at the first, which Quine develops ingeniously. To illustrate it, consider Quine's example (6) again:

Whoever walks rapidly, walks

Immediately, it can be seen that there is an open class of adverbs that can be substituted for 'rapidly' without endangering the validity of the argument. These are adverbs of manner, *e.g.*, 'slowly', 'quietly', 'carefully', and instrumental adverbs such as 'with a crutch', 'with a stick'; however, the class excludes sentence adverbs such as 'presumably', 'perhaps'. Now

Quine's solution is to introduce a new category of schematic letters, i.e. schematic letters for manner adverbs and instrumental adverbs, that enable one to capture what is common to the members of an open, but nevertheless grammatically well defined, class of arguments.

Independently Keenan and Faltz have developed a full blown theory of logical types for natural language (in Montague's spirit) and considerably enlarged the domain of logic by showing that the types containing the denotations of expressions subsumed under syntactic categories, such as adverbs, prepositions or adjective phrases, to mention just three of them, can be treated as the domain or range of *Boolean operations*. Once this has been established the inferential potential of a vast amount of constructions available in natural language can be accounted for. (Keenan & Faltz [1985])

Quine is sensitive to the fact that a *logically* valid argument is such in virtue of its form, i.e., an argument where only logical words occur essentially, as in 'John is a poet therefore John is a poet or $2+2=4$'. Some linguists obliterate the distinction between 'formal validity' and 'analyticity'. Katz, for instance, constructs a definition of 'semantic entailment' which puts among valid arguments inferences like 'John is a bachelor, therefore John is male' (Katz [1972], p. 24). Confirmation of this comes from the definition of *logical form* that Katz accepts: "Intensionalists understand the logical form of a sentence to consist of *every* property of the sentence that determines the role it plays in valid arguments" (Katz [1975], p. 76). But this account of logical form is far too liberal, incorporating as it does the *sense* of *no matter what* item occurs essentially in an argument. Katz fails to distinguish 'logically valid', i.e., an argument whose conclusion follows from its premisses in virtue of its logical form, from 'analytically valid', i.e., an argument whose conclusion follows from its premisses in virtue of the meanings of non-logical terms contained therein. That confusion is frequently made. It is already to be found in Moore's writings. In a famous paper he subsumes under the concept of entailment

... the sense in which the conclusion of a syllogism in Barbara follows from the two premisses, taken as one conjunctive proposition; or in which the proposition "This is coloured" follows from "This is red." (Moore [1922], p. 291)

Now since Quine has reduced the analytic-synthetic distinction to one of *degree*, he cannot accept a conception of logical form like Katz's, for it would put at risk the very notion of logical inference. It is, therefore, important for him to be able to clearly delineate the boundaries of logic, and, at the same time allow for possible enrichments of logic. His definition of logic built on the basis of the contrast between grammar and lexicon enables him to do this to a certain extent.

But, as was pointed out above, there exists another, more fashionable, way of extending the frontiers of logic, a method which consists of enriching the list of logical particles by incorporating new items. For example, to the grammatical constructions built up using the connectives ('and', 'or', 'if ... then ...', etc.) one might be tempted to add epistemic constructions such as 'knows that', 'believes that', so that one can account for the fact that

(10) If one knows that grass is green, then it is true that grass is green

is a logical truth in that the statement 'Grass is green' occurs vacuously in it. Føllesdal, for instance, has expressly demanded the right to extend logic in this way:

But first, is there such a thing as a logic of knowledge? Many philosophers would answer *no*. Still, it is easy to specify what the logic of knowledge is. Using Bolzano's old definition of logical truth, we can say that the logic of knowledge is the study of all phrases in which the only terms that occur *essentially* (to use Quine's phrase) are the logical terms of classical logic (statement logic, quantification theory, and identity theory), and expressions like 'knows that' and its cognates. (Føllesdal [1967], p. 1)

Quine, however, forbids the kind of extension that Føllesdal wants to carry out in his name, judging it undesirable: "Somehow 'believes that' and 'wishes that' seem too colorful to count as pure logical particles" (Quine, [1970c], p. 79). Here Quine seems to be concerned with a feature of logical terms which Ryle held to be their defining character:

Part of what characterizes the terms which do, on this view, carry inferences is that these terms or 'logical constants' are indifferent to subject matter, or are topic-neutral ... (Ryle [1954], p. 115)

So if (10) is raised to the status of a logical truth, the neutrality and universality stressed by Ryle is lost. Therefore, for Quine, 'epistemic logic' is improperly so called: it is more like the axiomatization of a particular theory, such as arithmetic, than predicate or propositional logic, and differs in this respect from the logic of adverbs that Quine, as we said, is ready to welcome side by side with predicate logic.

4. Recurrence and Synonymy

Quine claims to have given a purely extensional definition of logical truth. But Strawson has disputed this, maintaining for instance that

> Quine's characterization of logical truth can be made coherent, and made to do its job, only by implicit use of notions belonging to the group which he wishes to discredit. (Strawson [1957], p. 126)

Strawson's claim is that Quine's definition of logical truth *implicitly* appeals to the concept of synonymy, and so is only apparently better off in this respect than the definition of analyticity itself which does so *explicitly*. That an implicit appeal is made can be seen, Strawson thinks, if one reflects that on Quine's account a logical truth is a truth that remains true for all uniform substitutions of its non-logical terms. But this will give false results unless to the requirement of *uniformity*, that of *univocality* is added. For consider

(11)   All penguins are penguins.

Not all uniform substitutions on its non-logical terms preserve truth. The following sentence obtained in this way is ambiguous

(12)   All cranes are cranes.

Even ignoring figurative usages of language it clearly contains an equivocal term, 'crane', meaning either a bird of a certain sort, or a machine for lifting. Since, without a requirement of univocality, it is possible to take the first occurrence of 'crane' in the first sense, and the second in the second, (12) could be false, and so is no more a logical truth than

(13)   All birds are machines.

On the other hand, if a requirement of univocality is made, use has to be made of a concept belonging to the family to which *synonymity* belongs.
  To meet this objection it seems that one would have to give a purely extensional account of univocality, a seemingly impossible task. Nevertheless, Quine has a brilliant reply to Strawson (Quine [1968d], p. 296). Predicate calculus is known to be adequate and complete in the sense that all logically demonstrable sentences are true, and *vice-versa*. Imagine now

135

that certain predicate constants have been added to the calculus, including, for example, 'x is a crane'. Now if any of these are equivocal some demonstrable sentences of the language will become *false*, for instance

(14) $(\forall x)(x$ is a crane $\supset x$ is a crane$)$

will be false if the former occurrence of 'crane' is understood in one way and the other occurrence in the other way. So by contraposition if *all* the demonstrable sentences of the language are true, it contains no equivocal predicates. Thus, we have an extensional criterion of univocality applicable to any part of natural language that can be regimented into first order predicate calculus – the only part of interest to Quine.

Many, no doubt, will find this answer unsatisfactory complaining that "one wants to know how it is that we can paraphrase ordinary ambiguous English into the regimented language" (Deckert [1973], p. 55). But from Quine's point of view this objection seems misplaced. For he never claims that the object of paraphrasing a sentence into canonical notation is to preserve the sense it had in natural language. Part of his quarrel with the methods of analytic philosophers, after all, is that they rely on the notions of analyticity and synonymity.

Since language is an instrument, there can be no objection in principle to trying to improve it. So the kind of regimentation involved in paraphrase into canonical notation is not *a priori* objectionable. After all we have become familiar with the idea that grammatical theory can regiment our intuitions about grammaticality. As Chomsky writes:

That is, we may assume for this discussion that certain sequences of phonemes are definitely sentences, and that certain other sequences are definitely non-sentences. In many intermediate cases we shall be prepared to let the grammar itself decide, when the grammar is set up in the simplest way so that it includes the clear sentences and excludes the clear non-sentences. (Chomsky [1957], p. 14)

But if grammatical theory can do this with our intuitions about grammaticality, why should not logic be able to do the same with sentence-meanings?

5. Relations Between Logical Truths and Language

In a logical truth such as

(15) Either Othello loves Desdemona or Othello does not love Desdemona

the terms 'Othello', 'Desdemona' and 'loves' occur vacuously. Whether or not Othello loves Desdemona (15) is true. This may well suggest that (15) is true *independently* of what is the case. It is of course true that 'or' and 'not' occur essentially in (15), so that it is open to someone who accepts Quine's definition of a logical truth to argue that all sentences of the form (15) describe a very general structure of reality, and that is why they are true. But since Wittgenstein's *Tractatus* there have been few defenders of such an idea. Realist conceptions of logical truth have ceased to be fashionable; and the model for logical truth has become the tautology which says nothing about reality.

Many have been led to accept this view as a consequence of accepting a certain view of the way in which logical truths may be proved. Taking only their syntactical properties into consideration, they are shown to be derivable by a series of formal steps from a small number of sentences that constitute the axioms of the theory. These axioms, in turn, are thought of as being true *ex vi terminorum*, i.e., in virtue of the meanings of the words they contain. The *Principia Mathematica* axiom 'If p or p, then p' is, it would be argued, a sentence that becomes true once the meanings of its logical constants have been fixed; so that its truth value depends only on the meanings of those constants.

Seductive though this view is it can be attacked on the ground that the notion of dependence appealed to is itself unexplained. If, as Quine notes, by 'depends' one means 'depends logically' (i.e., 'is implied by'), then it is false that a logical truth is implied only by statements descriptive of the meanings of the terms they contain. Indeed since it is a logical truth that '$q \supset (p \supset q)$', every logical truth is materially implied by any statement whatever. As Quine writes: "Trivially, then, the logical truths are true by virtue of any circumstances you care to name – language, the world, anything" (Quine [1970c], p. 96). If the kind of generalized holism advocated in *Two Dogmas* is adopted, truths of logic are true *by virtue* of the experiences which impinge on the surface – i.e. true by virtue of a reality exterior to language. The fact that we can discover them by purely linguistic operations does not affect their nature, or their connection with reality.

At this point it might be claimed that to say that the truth of 'If either p or p, then p' depends on the meanings of 'or' and 'if... then', is not to say that it is *implied* by a statement descriptive of their meanings, but rather that to fix the meanings of the logical constants simply is, *at the same time*, to fix the meanings of the sentences in which they, and they alone, occur essentially. To do the first thing is *eo ipso* to do the second. In support of this it might be argued that the sense of '$(p \vee p) \supset p$' is fixed for us by a truth table that assigns it the value *True* both when p is true and p is false. In other words, '$(p \vee p) \supset p$' is true no matter what truth value p has. From which it is tempting to conclude that it is true independently of p's truth value, and so depends only on the meanings of 'or' and 'if... then'.

Note too that the substituents in a schema have to be statements if the result is to be a logical truth, and statements, by definition, are capable of truth or falsity. So an explanation by use of truth tables of the logical constants presupposes the concept of truth. We are thus led back to the conclusion that the concept of logical truth presupposes that of truth, as Quine's definition claims.

6. Model-Theoretic Versus Proof-Theoretic Conceptions of Logic

Quine's definition of logical truth is semantic: as he says "logic, like any science, has as its business the pursuit of truth" (Quine [1950], p. XI). But at the same time his will to avoid unwanted ontological commitments leads him to prefer syntactic accounts when possible. Thus, thanks to the completeness theorem for predicate calculus, we can demarcate the set of valid quantificational schema – "without [an] excursion through classes" (Quine [1950], p. 190) – as the set of statements demonstrable using the rules of first-order predicate calculus.

An example of Quine's tendency to avoid unnecessary ontological commitment is his definition of the validity of a schema. A schema, he maintains, is valid, if every uniform substitution of its schematic letters results in a true statement. This dispenses with the ontological commitments involved in the usual definition, *viz*, that a schema is valid if every *assignment* of a truth value, classes of individuals, classes of pairs of individuals, etc. ..., to its 0, 1, ... n-place schematic letters respectively results in a true statement. (Quine [1950], p. 190)

However, in an article appearing in 1968 "Logical Truth Revisited",

Hinman, Kim and Stich have given an example of a schema that is valid on Quine's account, but not on the traditional one. The schema is:

(16) $(\exists x)(\exists y)(Px \& Py \& x \neq y) \vee (\forall x) Px \vee (\forall x) \sim Px$

For consider a language L_1 containing all the apparatus of quantificational logic with identity and containing just one nonlogical atomic predicate, the one-place predicate P. Suppose further that at least two things are P and that at least two things are not P. (For concreteness we may think of P as an abbreviation of 'is red'). (Hinman, Kim, and Stich [1968], p. 498)

In (16) 'P' occurs vacuously since:

For each expression that may grammatically replace P must have as its extension one of four classes: the class of things that are P, the class of things that are not P, the null class, and the universal class. (Hinman, Kim and Stich [1968], p. 498)

The substitution for 'P' of a predicate having one of these four extensions leaves the truth of (16) intact. Indeed, if 'P' has red objects for its extension, then the first member of the disjunction if true for, by hypothesis, the universe contains at least two red objects. On the other hand if 'P' has those objects that are not red as its extension, then it is also true since there are at least two non-red objects. Moreover, if 'P' designates the universal class the second member of the disjunction is true, and if 'P' designates the null class, then the third disjunction is. Since a disjunction is true if at least one disjunct is true, (16) is true in every case. In other words, the schema is valid for Quine; but it isn't valid in the traditional sense, since it isn't satisfied by all models.

In our view it is possible to reply to this objection by exploiting a passage in *Philosophy of Logic* in which Quine added a further condition to the claim that the two definitions are equivalent. This claim is true, he writes, only "as long as our object language is reasonably rich: rich enough for elementary number theory" (Quine [1970c], p. 53). If this condition is satisfied, one can, thanks to the Löwenheim theorem, show that "if a schema comes out true under all substitutions of sentences of elementary number theory, it is satisfied by every model". (Quine [1970c], p. 54)

This enables Quine to avoid the thrust of the counterexample of Hinman *et al*. For the breakdown in equivalence of the two definitions that the counterexample brings to light can be attributed to the *excessive poverty* of the language L_1 that is in question. In a language rich enough to express elementary arithmetic, this breakdown would not occur, for in such a language there will be a predicate P of which it will not be true that for each of its four possible extensions (the class of things that are P, the complement of this class, the null class and the universal class) the schema is true. Any sentence that comes out true under all substitutions of sentences, in such a language, will also be satisfied by all models and conversely. (Quine [1970c], pp. 53–54)

In "What is Logic?" I. Hacking proposes a definition of logic in terms of proof and not of truth: "... logic is the science of deduction" (Hacking [1979], p. 290). The interest of Hacking's proof-theoretic definition is that it makes possible a convincing justification of the *boundary* that Quine establishes between logic and non-logic. Hacking's definition, for example, enables one to see why second order logic, and modal logic, do not have the same status as first order non-modal logic, although deviant logics, such as intuitionistic logic, do. Hacking has, as it were, discovered the principle of Quine's demarcation procedures, and succeeded in making them immune to the charge of arbitrariness better than Quine himself succeeded in doing.

A further merit of Hacking's definition is that it gives a sense to the logicist programme, understood as Quine intends it to be, that is not as a way of providing foundations for mathematics, but as a way of explaining the nature of necessary truths. Finally, Hacking makes room for the insight that necessary truths rest on the *sense* of certain words, *without* conceding to mathematicians the power to create truth by *convention*. Thus, once Hacking's proposal is accepted, a constellation of Quine's philosophical positions is found to be unified and justified.

Hacking takes as his key notion not that of logical consequence, which is a semantic notion, but the syntactical notion of deducibility, such as that isolated and presented in a pure form in the Gentzen sequent calculus. He then sets out the characteristic properties of the classical relation of deducibility, which present themselves in a tangible way in rules that Gentzen calls structural, by contrast with the operational rules used to introduce the logical constants. It is because they depart from certain of the conditions codified in the structural rules that the deducibility relations obtaining in modal logic, or type theory supplemented by the axiom of reducibility, cannot claim the same status as non-modal first order logic.

VI
Deviant Logics

1. Quine's Oscillations Between Conservatism and Liberalism in Logic

Quine oscillates between a liberal and a conservative position on the subject of deviant logic. Before trying to settle the issue, it is indispensable to review the most significant statements that Quine has made on the subject.

The liberal position is at its clearest in the following passage from *Two Dogmas*:

> ... no statement is immune to revision. Revision even of the logical law of excluded middle has been proposed as a means of simplifying quantum mechanics ... (Quine [1951a], p. 43)

This is echoed in *Philosophy of Logic*:

> Logic is in principle no less open to revision than quantum mechanics or the theory of relativity. The goal is, in each, a world system – in Newton's phrase – that is as smooth and simple as may be and that nicely accommodates observations around the edges. If revisions are seldom proposed that cut so deep as to touch logic, there is a clear enough reason for that: the maxim of minimum mutilation. (Quine [1970c], p. 100)

But in other passages Quine draws so narrow a line between the doctrinal element in logic (the laws), and the conceptual one (the meaning of the constants), that revision becomes impossible in fact. In *Word and Object* for instance he says:

> Again, when someone espouses a logic whose laws are ostensibly contrary to our own, we are ready to speculate that he is just giving some familiar old vocables ('and', 'or', 'not', 'all', etc.) new meanings. (Quine [1960a], p. 59)

And in *Philosophy of Logic* Quine comments as follows on a dialogue between a revolutionary, who rejects the principle of contradiction, and a conservative trying to make him change his mind:

My view of this dialogue is that neither party knows what he is talking about. They think they are talking about negation, '∼', 'not'; but surely the notation ceased to be recognizable as negation when they took to regarding some conjunction of the form '$p . \sim p$' as true, and stopped regarding such sentences as implying all others. Here, evidently, is the deviant logician's predicament: when he tries to deny the doctrine he only changes the subject. (Quine [1970c], p. 81)

These last two claims put the thesis of the revisability of logic at risk in two ways: on the one hand, it can be said that the revised logic does not differ in *substance* from the old one, but only in its *notation*. From this point of view, the two claims in question can be construed as trivializing the enterprise of revision. According to another possible interpretation of these claims, which is no more favourable to the idea of revision than is the first, there is a way of changing a logic and not only its notation, but, it is added, the new logic is simply *incommensurable* with the old one. If then one changes the logical laws, one changes the *senses* of the logical constants, and if to change the senses of the constants is to change the subject, then there is no *contact*, and hence no *conflict*, between classical and deviant logic. This diminishes interest in revision.

2. Against the Incommensurability Thesis

In *Deviant Logic* Susan Haack used several arguments to counter the claim that the change in meaning of the logical constants generates a sort of incommensurability which makes *conflict* impossible.

First she offers the following astute counter-example (Haack [1974], p. 9). Consider a deviant logician who denies

$$(p \vee q) \supset (\sim p \supset q)$$

but who gives to '∨' the interpretation which the classical logician gives to '∧'. One can argue that the deviant and the classical logician who respectively deny and accept this formula as a theorem are talking about a *different subject*: the former talks about the sentence which logically follows from a conjunction and denies that the formula obtained by negating the first conjunct and substituting a conditional for the sign of conjunction is among them. The classical logician talks about the sentence which follows from a disjunction and claims that the formula obtained by negating the first disjunct and substituting a conditional for the disjunction sign is among them.

Yet, even though the deviant and the classical logician can be described as talking about different propositions, as they give different truth-table interpretations to the symbol '$\vee$', and hence to the formula '$(p \vee q) \supset (\sim p \supset q)$', they are nevertheless *also* in conflict, because even on the classical reading the deviant logician is in conflict with the classical logician who besides taking '$(p \vee q) \supset (\sim p \supset q)$' as a theorem, takes '$(p \wedge q) \supset (\sim p \supset q)$' as a theorem too.

Admittedly if one discards truth table interpretation and maintains that the meaning of the constants is given only by the axioms and rules, any sets of axioms + rules which are not equipollent will give rise to incommensurability. This, however, reduces Quine's claim to the status of a mere stipulative delimitation of what counts as the 'subject matter' of logic.

Even if one concedes that the meanings of the connectives are given by the axioms and rules of the system, as Quine said they were, the conclusion that deviant logics are not genuinely rivals of classical logic, but rather theories dealing with another subject, hardly follows when there is "such a degree of overlap" (S. Haack [1974], p. 13) between the allegedly incommensurable logics, as is the case with Birkoff and von Neumann's logic for quantum mechanics. In this case, I would side with S. Haack and say that there is "no clear answer to the question, whether there is real rivalry".

Let us then acknowledge that the separation between real and apparent rivalry is a fuzzy one. Deviancy comes in different degrees. The question arises as to how we can assess this deviancy. Recent developments in a highly specialized field – quantum logic – indicate that deviancy cannot be confined to syntax (axioms, rules) but that it transfers to a very deep level of *semantics*. For instance, M.L. Dalla Chiara shows that the *Lindenbaum-property* is violated in quantum mechanics.

The Lindenbaum-property is violated, because there are non contradictory sentences... which cannot be extended to any non contradictory and *complete* set of sentences T (such that for any sentence β, either $\beta \in T$ or $\sim \beta \in T$). (Dalla Chiara [forthcoming])

S. Haack claims that the sort of extreme conservatism in logic which Quine advocated in *Philosophy of Logic* is inconsistent with the rejection of the analytic-synthetic distinction in so far as extreme conservatism in logic presupposes the possibility of drawing a distinction between disagreement in belief and semantic misunderstanding.

However, the *Philosophy of Logic* thesis is that there can be no such thing as a real, but only an apparent, change of logic. It is worth stressing, also, how important a change is made in Quine's philosophy by his acceptance of this thesis. For it commits him to admitting a distinction between linguistic change and factual change which it was one of the crucial points of ['Two Dogmas'] to deny. Indeed Grice and Strawson, in ['In the defence of a Dogma'], take it that the concession of this distinction would be a major advance against Quine. (S. Haack [1974], p. 15)

I do not think, however, that Quine's shift towards conservatism threatens his views on the analytic-synthetic dichotomy. Quine might use the following argument to support the privileged status he gives to logic. When engaged in radical translation or even in conversation with members of our linguistic community – indeterminacy begins at home – we should apply the ethical principle of charity, i.e. interpret language in a way which maximizes agreement. To leave logic unaffected is thus a reasonable policy, since logic pervades all language in so far as it is topic neutral. This way of vindicating the consistency of Quine's position would fail however, if we abandoned the concept of universal logic, in favour of logical pluralism.

Logical pluralism which denies the existence of a unique logical framework, has its proponents. Thus Madame Février wrote in 1951: "There is no unique logic independent of content, but in each domain a logic turns out to be adequate" (Destouches-Février [1951], p. 88). And Apostel, noting in *Matière et Forme* (1974) that the past is closed whilst the future is open, proposes that, because this is so, a different logic should be applied to them:

If the past is radically different from the future, and if they blend in the present, then the existential quantifications in a causal conditional's antecedent should be radically different from those in the consequent, and the relation of production itself should have an heterogeneous ontological status ... As, however, we ought to be able to express references to different moments of time in a single language L ... it is necessary to include these different moments whilst preserving their proper status. One way ... to do this would be to describe the past with a bivalent logic and the future with a trivalent one. (Apostel [1974], vol. I, p. 52)

Quantum logic is a good candidate. It is in an even better position than epistemic logic whose key-concepts of 'knows' and 'believes' are described by Quine as too 'colourful', i.e., too topic-dependent to be raised to the status of 'logic'. The specificity of Quantum logic lies in the semantics of connectives and quantifiers and also in the semantics of descriptions. This last point was recently made by M.L. Dalla Chiara in "The Relevance of Quantum Logic in the Domain of Non-Classical Logics":

> ... at the semantical level, the notion of truth is usually constructed in such a way that a *semantical richness* property holds: $\exists x\alpha$ is true iff there exists at least one individual of the domain which satisfies α. However, this property breaks down in first-order Quantum logic, where it may even happen that: $\exists!!\ x\alpha$ (there exists exactly one x which is α) is true, while there is no precise individual in the domain that satisfies the property expressed by α! This situation renders ... very problematic the possibility of a reasonable description-theory in Quantum logic. But, in spite of its apparent logical disagreeability, such a behaviour of the concept of individual seems to fit very well with characteristic features of particular objects in microphysics. (Dalla Chiara [forthcoming])

Recall that Quine brought microphysics to bear on his choice of ontology. This is fully in accordance with his well-known physicalistic standpoint. However if Quine wants to adjust his logic to physics, he may have had to give up his claim that names can be eliminated in favour of descriptions.

3. For and Against Revisionism in Logic

We shall see later that Quine has tried to resolve the conflict between his views and to give a more satisfying account of deviance in the *Roots of Reference*. Before looking at his new views on deviance, however, it is worth asking whether, when everything is taken into account, it is so important to save the thesis of the revisability of logic. Certain logicians doubt that it is; for example, Geach, who vigorously defends a conservative position, writes:

> Logic must be kept rigid, come what may in the way of physical theories; for only so can it serve as a crowbar to overthrow unsatisfactory theories. Lavoisier remarked that the phlogistonists ascribed different and indeed incompatible properties to phlogiston in order to explain different experimental results; what a good thing there were not then logicians prepared to bend logic in the interests of the phlogiston theory – to say that these were 'complementary' accounts of phlogiston, both true so long as you did not combine them. (Geach [1965], p. 323 as quoted in R.J. Haack [1978], p. 249)

These objections contain some important truths: but it is perfectly possible to concede them without giving up the thesis of revisability. One can grant that in an argument some logic is always presupposed, and, for that reason, is not on that occasion in dispute. But it has at that point only a *provisional immunity*; and like that given to parliamentarians during the period of their mandate it can be lifted. Logic is needed, even to criticize logic, but this does not confer any priority on it. At each moment, it is necessary that there exists a logical framework as a condition of a theory's being inconsistent either with experience or internally, but it does not follow that there is just one framework that exists at all moments.

In 'Two Dogmas', Quine did not even concede that. He put statements (of the web of belief) and logical laws on the same footing:

Reevaluation of some statements [of the web of belief] entails reevaluation of others, because of their logical interconnections – the logical laws being in turn simply certain further statements in the system, certain further elements of the field. (Quine [1951], p. 42)

This statement contains a confusion which Priest, as we have seen (see Chapter I, Section 4), has brought to the foreground:

A statement in the system may be a statment corresponding to a logical interconnection but it cannot *be* the logical connection on pain of infinite regress. (Priest [1979], p. 293)

Now that the points at issue between the revisability thesis and the conservative position have been reviewed, the time has come to choose one of the two positions between which Quine oscillates, and to justify that choice. This is what S. Haack has done in her book *Deviant Logic*. In it she advances arguments which seem conclusive to us, in favour of revisability. In particular she shows that "it is not in principle impossible that developments in physics should give rise to a need for a change of logic" (S. Haack [1974], p. 167). Moreover, she attacks the kind of logical conservatism found in Quine's writings. Her criticism shows that Quine's arguments for universal agreement on classical tautologies rested on two assumptions:

(a) the principle of maximizing agreement;

(b) the adoption of assent and dissent as behavioural coordinates.

However, these preliminary assumptions effectively prejudge the question. The adoption of three behavioural coordinates, assent, dissent and puzzlement would have made another interpretation of the native's responses possible, and one, moreover, which would have allowed us to attribute to him a non-classical logic in which 'p or not-p' is not a logical truth.

4. Verdict Functions Versus Truth-Functions

In *Roots of Reference* Quine freed himself from the assumption of a dichotomy between *assent* and *dissent*, replacing it with a trichotomy between *assent*, *dissent*, and *abstention*, thus showing S. Haack to be right about the imputation of assumption (b) to him:

A contrast thus emerges between truth functions and something more primitive, *verdict functions*. Verdict logic is three-valued, the three verdicts being assent, dissent and abstention. (Quine [1974], p. 77)

The discovery of these verdict functions, which are more primitive than the truth functions, led Quine to modify two of his earlier positions. The first concerns the status of propositional connectives: in *Word and Object* he maintains that the sense of these logical terms can be grasped by observation of behaviour. Connectives, like observation sentences, therefore have a stimulus meaning. They escape also from the effects of indeterminacy of translation, differing in this respect from quantifiers interpreted objectually. The latter, indeed, can only be understood and translated thanks to the use of analytical hypotheses, and are, therefore, subject to indeterminacy.

From the *Roots of Reference* onwards Quine withdraws these privileges from truth functions, or at least from some of them. If negation is both a truth function and a verdict function, conjunction is, Quine argues, only a truth function, there being no completely defined verdict function in this case:

AND Q	assent	abstain	dissent
P			
assent	AS	AB	DIS
abstain	AB	?	DIS
dissent	DIS	DIS	DIS

He comments as follows:

> Conjunction has its blind spot, however, where neither component commands assent nor dissent. There is no direct way of mastering this quarter. In some such cases the conjunction commands dissent and in others it commands nothing. This sector is mastered only later in theory-laden ways. Where the components are 'It is a mouse' and 'It is a chipmunk', and neither is affirmed nor denied, the conjunction will still be denied. But where the components are 'It is a mouse' and 'It is in the kitchen', and neither is affirmed nor denied, the conjunction will perhaps be left in abeyance. (Quine [1974], p. 76–77)

The discovery of verdict functions has a second consequence, which is, this time, directly relevant to our subject matter, and which, in Quine's view, enables him to mitigate the rigour of his conservatism. Verdict functions "can be learned by induction from observation of verdictive behaviour" (Quine [1974], p. 78). By contrast, truth functions and two valued logic are theoretical constructions, *under-determined* by observation, of such a sort that different theories, namely, *different logics*, are compatible with the data of verdictive behaviour:

> Some theorists, notably the intuitionists, favor another logic [than the classical one] and there is nothing in the observable circumstances of our utterances that need persuade them to assign meaning to our two-valued scheme. (Quine [1974], p. 78)

This liberalization is, however, limited: it concerns, for example, the principle of excluded middle '$p \vee \sim p$', but not the rule of addition '$p \supset p \vee q$'. There are, therefore, two sorts of logical laws, those that are understood when the logical constants are learned – as is the case with the law of addition – and those that are not, like the law of excluded middle. The first kind can be called 'analytic' in a new sense of the term that we will represent, following S. Haack, by 'analytique'. A decisive step has thus been taken: in the case of *synthetic* logical laws, such as that of excluded middle, it is possible to disassociate the truth of a law from the sense of the logical constants that it contains, and, therefore, to accept the latter but deny the former. Henceforth, revision is possible for laws of this sort.

However, it seems that this moderate solution is untenable, and that, if one opens the way for the revision of some logical principles, one should do so for all. In "Analyticity and Logical Truth in the *Roots of Reference*" ([1977], pp. 121, 143) S. Haack marshalled considerations that show that no principle is 'analytique', that is, is immune from all possibility of revision. The argument is as follows: when one establishes correlations between verdict and truth-tables, there is always a way of doing this of such a kind that any principle might fail to be uniformly designated in some eventual truth-tables consistent with the verdict tables. In other words, there is always a way of correlating the tables of truth functions with those of verdict functions that degrades any logical principle whatsoever to the rank of a 'synthetic principle'. This Quine had not grasped because he had considered only one level of theoreticity involved in truth functions, namely, that in which, by a stipulation, the logician fills in the *gap* that existed in the middle of the verdict-table. Quine had thus lost sight of a second 'element of theoreticity', namely the correlating of verdict-tables with truth-tables.

It is disputable whether Quine has not gone far enough in his concessions on the subject of logical deviance, as S. Haack believes, or whether he has gone too far, given certain other of his theses which he still retains, as A. Berger believes (Berger [1980], pp. 259–277). We shall not try to settle this issue here. We shall simply observe that the very existence of opposing objections to Quine's position on the matter bears witness to the inner tensions and strains which exert themselves in Quine's views on the subject.

VII
Quantified Modal Logic

1. From Intensionality to Referential Opacity

The *principle of extensionality* is widely espoused by logicians using logic as a tool for the analysis of mathematical reasoning. A very clear formulation of this principle can be found in Russell's *Inquiry into Meaning and Truth*:

The principle of extensionality has two parts:

I. The truth-value of any function of a proposition depends only upon the truth-value of the argument, i.e. if p and q are both true or both false, then any sentence containing p remains true or false, as the case may be, if q is substituted for p.

II. The truth-value of any function of a function depends only on the extension of the function, i.e. if whenever Φx is true, ψx is true, and vice versa, then any sentence about the function Φ remains true or false as the case may be, if ψ is substituted for Φ. (Russell [1940], p. 168)

These two formulations can be fused into a single one if we construe statements as 0-place predicates. The unified principle of extensionality can be formulated in this way

materially equivalent sentences or coextensive predicates are interchangeable *salva veritate*

and rendered formally as follows (1), where $n \geqslant 0$:

(1) $\quad [\Phi x_1 \ldots x_n \equiv \psi x_1 \ldots x_n] \supset [f(\Phi x_1 \ldots x_n) \equiv f(\psi x_1 \ldots x_n)]$.

It was soon recognized that the principle of extensionality or the principle of truth-functionality which was part I in Russell's formulation did not hold in a language rich enough to contain, in addition to mathematical terms, *modal* constructions such as 'necessarily p', 'p strictly implies q' or doxastic constructions such as 'A believes p'. The latter construction is mentioned as an example of a non-truth-functional construction by Russell and White-

150

head in appendix C to *Principia Mathematica* (Whitehead & Russell [²1927], pp. 401–402, second edition) and the former ones are mentioned as illustrations of the same phenomenon – which we shall call 'intensionality' from now on – by Lewis and Langford [1932] in their *Symbolic Logic*.

In his early paper "Notes on Existence and Necessity" [1943], Quine makes a much stronger claim. He contends that modal contexts violate not only the principle of extensionality, but also Leibniz's principle of substitutivity of identicals which says that substitution of identicals does not alter the truth-value of the sentence. Formally, the principle reads as follows:

(2) $(\forall x)(\forall y)(x = y \supset \Phi_x \equiv \Phi_y)$ [1]

Leibniz himself knew that his principle did not hold in all contexts (H. Burkhardt [1980], p. 231 ff). Let us focus on a context in which Leibniz' principle fails for obvious reasons: the context of quotes. Clearly the following argument is invalid:

(3) 'Cicero' has six letters
     Cicero = Tully
     'Tully' has six letters.

The law of universal instantiation

(4) $(\forall x) Fx \vdash Fy$ [2]

and the law of existential generalization

(5) $Fy \vdash (\exists x) Fx$ [3]

are not valid either in that context. The reason for the failure of substitutivity of identicals and for the miscarriage of quantification is obvious: terms (i.e., proper names, definite descriptions, individual variables) within a context of quotes do not occur *designatively*. It would be

---

[1] If Φ_y is obtained by putting y instead of x when x and y are coreferential (designate identical individuals), Φ_y is equivalent to Φ_x.
[2] From 'all x are F', you may infer 'y is F'.
[3] From 'y is F', you may infer 'there is at least an x such that x is F'.

absurd to claim that they do so, just as it would be absurd to claim that the noun 'cat' occurs within the noun 'cattle'. Clearly 'cat' is a phonetic but not a semantic part of 'cattle'.

This is indeed common knowledge. Quine, however, goes much further and says quite bluntly that

> the ... modes of intensional composition of statements are, in fact, subject to the same defects as the context of quotes ...
> It follows that the context 'necessarily ...' at least in the analytic sense which we are considering, is similar to the context of single quotes and to the contexts 'is unaware that ...', 'believes that ...' etc. ...
> It does not admit pronouns which refer to quantifiers anterior to the context. (Quine [1943], p. 123)

Whitehead, Russell and C.I. Lewis taught us that modal-contexts and belief-contexts were intensional, i.e. substitution of materially equivalent sentences or coextensive predicates sometimes results in a change of truth-value of the context. Frege taught us that in these contexts references *change*, i.e., that referring expressions have *indirect* reference. Quine makes a much bolder claim: he contends that these contexts are opaque in much the same way as is the context of quotation. A context is *opaque* when the substitution of identicals sometimes alters the truth-value. Violation of Leibniz's law generates opacity. Violation of the principle of extensionality generates intensionality.

Quine's *reduction of intensionality* to *referential opacity* is convincing if we treat the object language operator on statements (6),

(6)   Necessarily ——————,

as a notational variant of the meta-linguistic predicate (7),

(7)   '——————' is analytic.

But subject to the above mentioned proviso, the reduction is not only convincing, it is also *trivial*, since

(8)   '——————' is analytic,

makes 'is analytic' a predicate applying to quotations.

Admittedly, Quine did not stop here. He also considered modal expressions construed as object language operators on closed or on open sentences, such as,

(9) Necessarily $9 > 7$,

(10) $\exists x \, N(x > 7)$,

respectively, and he developed an argument for which Barwise and Perry coined the expression "slingshot argument" (Barwise & Perry, [1981a], p. 387–403). The slingshot argument is designed to prove that in these cases of deeper 'modal involvement' also intensional opacity *comes very close* to reducing to referential opacity, although it does not do so in the end.

In order to establish that intensionality coincides with referential opacity, we have to prove two statements:

(11) *referential opacity* entails *intensionality*, and

(12) *intensionality* entails *referential opacity*.

The first statement is not at all controversial. We should therefore concentrate on (12) or on (13) which is obtained from (12) by contraposition:

(13) *referential transparency* entails *extensionality*.

It is (13) which Quine tried to support using an argument inspired by Church which is as follows:
Let us start with the propositional context

(14) $F(p)$,

which *ex hypothesi* is referentially transparent. Quine contends that even if the only permissible substitutions for 'p' are statements *logically* equivalent to it, if we assume transparency, we can show that '$F(p)$' is equivalent to '$F(q)$', for an arbitrary 'q'. In other words, referential transparency acts like a Trojan horse which destroys intensionality.

Let us take 'Snow is white' for 'p'. As Quine observes, "if 'p' is true, then the conjunction '$x = \Lambda \,\&\, p$' is true of one and only one object x, viz, the empty class Λ" (Quine [1953b], p. 163). Hence, the following biconditional is valid, i.e. it expresses a logical equivalence

153

(15) $\models p \equiv [\{\Lambda\} = \{x : x = \Lambda \& p\}]$.

Let us take 'grass is green' for 'q'.
By the same reasoning

(16) $\models q \equiv [\{\Lambda\} = \{x : x = \Lambda \& q\}]$.

But since "... classes, properly so-called, are one and the same if their members are the same – regardless of whether that sameness be a matter of logical proof or of historical accident" (Quine [1953b], p. 164), we can state the following identity statement

(17) $\{x : x = \Lambda \& p\} = \{\Lambda\} = \{x : x = \Lambda \& q\}$

and then apply Leibniz's law.
Hence, from

(18) $F(p)$ we can derive successively

(19) $F[\{\Lambda\} = \{x : x = \Lambda \& p\}]$

(20) $F[\{\Lambda\} = \{x : x = \Lambda \& q\}]$

(21) $F(q)$

Quine's argument holds for *any* propositional context, and thus *also for 'N' put in the F-position*. The conclusion is calamitous for modal logic. We seem to be unavoidably condemned to either renouncing referential transparency, which is required if we want a well behaved quantification theory, or to retaining referential transparency and to admitting that all modal distinctions collapse. Thus Quine's argument seems to completely undermine the alleged quantified modal logic by showing that it is *either meaningless or non modal*. Let us try to assess the strength of this argument.

2. From the Slingshot Argument to Essentialism

Quine, himself does not claim to have conclusively established the meaninglessness of quantified modal logic. He does not say that *intensionality* without *referential* opacity is impossible. He merely says that it is "less easy than one at first supposes".

In the sixties, Føllesdal pushed the matter much further and obtained a very important result: he established that intensionality is consistent with referential transparency, provided certain conditions are fulfilled. There are several alternative conditions and each one of them is sufficient, on its own, to enable us to salvage modal logic. In his dissertation, Føllesdal mentioned three of these conditions. We shall examine only the second and the third.

Føllesdal's second condition is this:

We permit some singular terms to appear in well-formed expressions of our modal system, viz. those expressions μ which satisfy the condition

$\ulcorner(\exists\beta)\,N\,(\forall\alpha)\,(\alpha\mu\text{'s} \equiv .\,\alpha = \beta)\urcorner.$[1]

Among these singular terms there may well be descriptions and class abstracts. (Føllesdal, [1961], p. 99)

Føllesdal's third condition reads as follows:

We use a full theory of descriptions. Descriptions are eliminated by standard Russellian contextual definitions. Thus e.g. $\ulcorner(\cap\alpha)\Phi = \beta\urcorner$[2] expands into $\ulcorner(\forall\alpha)(\Phi\alpha \equiv .\,\alpha = \beta)\urcorner$ i.e. any α who Φ-ies is identical with β. We do, however, not treat a description $\ulcorner(\cap\alpha)\Phi\urcorner$ as a name unless the supporting lemma

$\ulcorner(\exists\beta)\,N(\forall\alpha)(\Phi\alpha \equiv .\,\alpha = \beta)\urcorner$

is at hand. (Føllesdal [1961], p. 99)

Notice that Føllesdal limits the stock of singular *terms* but not the stock of objects. Limiting the stock of objects by alloting *intensional* referents to singular terms occurring within the scope of a modal operator, would be both ineffectual, as Quine has shown, and harmful. It would be harmful since, to borrow Lauener's example, it would turn the following sentence

(22) $(\exists x)\,[x > y\,\&\,Nx > y]$,

---

[1] i.e. There is an individual β, such that necessarily for all α, α satisfies the predicate μ if and only if α is identical with β.
[2] i.e. the unique individual α which satisfies the predicate φ is identical with the individual β.

into a meaningless expression because the variable 'x' ranges over extensional entities (individuals) the first time it occurs in the matrix, and over intensional entities (individual concepts) the second time.

If we adopt Føllesdal's solution, we rescue modal distinctions: co-extensive open sentences such as '$x = \sqrt{x} + \sqrt{x} + \sqrt{x} \neq \sqrt{x}$' and 'there are exactly x planets' cannot be interchanged in modal contexts *salva veritate*. Hence the following argument (23) is invalid as indeed it should be.

(23) $(\forall x) N (x = \sqrt{x} + \sqrt{x} + \sqrt{x} \neq \sqrt{x} . \supset . x > 7)$

$(\forall x) \{[(x = \sqrt{x} + \sqrt{x} + \sqrt{x} \neq \sqrt{x} . \supset . x > 7)] \equiv$
(there are exactly x planets $\supset . x > 7)\}$

therefore $(\forall x) N$ (there are exactly x planets $\supset x > 7)$.

On the other hand, co-referential singular terms are interchangeable *salva veritate* in modal contexts providing they satisfy the conditions (2) or (3) specified above. The following argument (24) is therefore valid:

(24) $N(9 > 7)$,

$9 = (\cap x)$ (x numbers the planets),

$(\exists y) N (\forall x)$ (x numbers the planets $\equiv x = y$),

therefore $N [(\cap x)$ (x numbers the planets) $> 7]$.

If we interpret the object language expression

(25) Np,

as the metalanguage expression

(26) 'p' is true in all possible worlds,

in accordance with Leibniz[1] (Couturat [1903]), Bayart ([1958], pp. 28–45), Kanger ([1957]), Hintikka, ([1961], pp. 110–128), Kripke ([1959], pp. 1–14), etc., we can say very clearly what Føllesdal's second and third solutions amount to. They amount in his words, to limiting

---

[1] 'Et hae sunt aeterne veritatis, nec tantum obtinebunt, dum stabit Mundus, set etiam obtinuissent, si DEUS alia ratione Mundum creâsset'.

our stock of definite singular terms... by keeping only those of them which refer to the same extensional object in all possible worlds ... (Føllesdal [1961], p. 116)

The number 9 is greater than 7 in all possible worlds, and by the same token is the same entity in all possible worlds whether it be referred to by the singular name '9' or by the definite description 'the number of the planets'. Once this piece of information has been added by introducing an appropriate lemma, the argument (27) holds:

(27) $N(9 > 7)$,

$9 = (\cap x)(nb.pl.x)$

$N((\cap x)(nb.pl.x) > 7)$

There is, however, a price to be paid for this result. We have to abandon the views of Carnap and C.I. Lewis for whom 'necessarily greater than seven' applies to the number nine only as designated by 'nine' but not as designated by 'the number of planets'. Abandoning Carnap's and Lewis' view on the matter amounts to claiming that nine is necessarily greater than seven regardless of the way in which nine is referred to. According to Føllesdal this move commits us to Aristotelian essentialism as Quine thought (Quine [1953c], pp. 155–156; [1953b], p. 175).

... Aristotelian essentialism is just what the unrestricted substitutivity of identity in modal contexts amounts to; if an attribute is necessary of an object, it is necessary of the object *regardless of the way in which the object is referred to*.
... To make sense of Aristotelian essentialism and to make sense of open sentences with an 'N' prefixed are one and the same problem ... (Føllesdal, [1961], p. 120)

3. On Essentialism

Essentialism contains an irrational element, which is revealed by the way in which it arbitrarily classes properties of objects, raising some to the rank of essential properties, and degrading others to that of accidental properties. Quine, of course, in no way criticizes those who distinguish between an object's essential and accidental traits in *relation* to the way in which that object is specified; but he has no time at all for the 'favouritism' shown by those who claim to be able to draw this distinction absolutely. The point is clearly made in *Word and Object*:

> Perhaps I can evoke the appropriate sense of bewilderment as follows. Mathematicians may conceivably be said to be necessarily rational and not necessarily two-legged; and cyclists necessarily two-legged and not necessarily rational. But what of an individual who counts among his eccentricities both mathematics and cycling? Is this concrete individual necessarily rational and contingently two-legged or vice versa? Just insofar as we are talking referentially of the object, with no special bias toward a background grouping of mathematicians as against cyclists or vice versa, there is no semblance of sense in rating some of his attributes as necessary and others as contingent. Some of his attributes count as important and others as unimportant, yes; some as enduring and others as fleeting; but none as necessary or contingent. (Quine, [1960a], p. 199)

Quine's objection was considered in 1967 by Ruth Barcan Marcus, the author of the first full blown system of quantified modal logic (QM). Ruth Barcan Marcus observes that although quantified modal logic presupposes the *meaningfulness* of aristotelian essentialism, it does *not* enable us to prove the *truth* of aristotelian essentialism:

> The question remains whether attributes of the sort which Quine discusses, e.g. two-leggedness, could be among the provably essential attributes of QM. Clearly they cannot ... (Barcan Marcus [1967], p. 95)

Terence Parsons continued the discussion and obtained another significant result: not only has QM no essential sentence as a theorem, but also QM cannot yield the proof of an essential sentence even if it is supplemented by some non-modal premiss. To prove that "[the system QM] together with some obvious and uncontroversial non-modal facts" does not entail that "some [essentialist] sentence be true" (T. Parsons [1969], p. 78) Parsons showed that QM admits a maximal model, i.e., one that contains for every consistent set of non-modal sentences a world in which they are true, that is to say a world in which the facts of this world hold, and no essential sentence is true.

Neither Barcan Marcus' nor Parsons' important results succeeded in allaying Quine's qualms. They have had, however, a significant effect which has passed unnoticed: they forced Quine to change his strategy and to search for another criticism against QM The trouble is, however, that this new criticism, as I shall show later, has a more restricted scope than the former.

Before showing this, let us first examine Quine's revised criticism. Quine wants to establish that QM is marred by essentialism. What is new is that he now locates essentialism at a *deeper level*. He claims that commitment to the truth of essentialism is unavoidable as soon as one has acknowledged the possibility of identifying individuals across possible worlds:

> Talk of possible worlds is a graphic way of waging the essentialist philosophy, but it is only that; it is not an explication. Essence is needed to identify an object from one possible world to another. (Quine, [1977b], p. 118)

One should observe, here, that Quine imputes to possible world semantics a version of essentialism which is *much stronger* than the one required by quantified modal logic. Føllesdal brings out the difference between these two notions of essentialism quite clearly in the following passage:

> The argument I have outlined shows that *if* an object has a necessary property, it has to have this property regardless of how the object is referred to. The argument does not show that any object in our universe of discourse has to have some non-trivial essential property, ... by which it can be identified. (Føllesdal, [forthcoming])

At least two interpretations of Aristotelian essentialism are possible:

(a) A property necessarily belongs to an object if the object has it *regardless of* how the object is referred to (weaker version);

(b) a property necessarily belongs to an object if the object has it *by virtue of* its essence, i.e., of a non trivial property by which it can be identified (stronger version).

Quine surreptitiously *leaps* from the weaker to the stronger version. Hence it is no surprise to hear him deplore the fact that possible world semantics has *displaced*, rather than *dissipated*, the fog which surrounded quantified modal logic:

> When modal logic has been paraphrased in terms of such notions as possible world or rigid designator, where the displaced fog settles is on the question when to identify objects between worlds, or when to treat a designator as rigid ... (Quine [1972], pp. 492–493)

To block Quine's move, one has to show that neither the *semantical* task of defining the notion of rigid designator nor the *epistemological* task of supplying criteria for identification of individuals across possible worlds requires the *metaphysical* doctrine of (strong) Aristotelian essentialism.

4. On Genuine Singular Terms

According to Føllesdal, genuine singular terms (rigid designators) have a sense which is determined by reference, "in an interplay with our theories of the world and our conception of how we gain knowledge and how we are likely to go wrong, in our perception and in our reasoning" (Føllesdal [forthcoming]). This sense is designed to ensure – but does not always succeed in ensuring – "that the term keeps on referring to what it presently refers to through the vicissitudes of increased insight and scientific changes".

On this account, the definitions of the notions of 'genuine singular term' and 'rigid designator' do not involve the concept of possible world. As Føllesdal observes

the notion of a genuine singular term is not fundamentally a modal notion, it is not a notion that requires appeal to necessity or essentialism. (Føllesdal [*ibid.*])

5. Identification of Individuals Across Possible Worlds

Hintikka has suggested that one might conceive identification of an object across possible worlds in the light of a more familiar operation: the operation of reidentifying an individual across successive moments of time. When identification across moments of time is at stake, the relevant criteria depend on what the object is. The relevant criteria of identification are continuity of displacement, continuity of deformation, and continuity of chemical change.

Quine, however, points to a crucial difference between identification through time and identification across possible worlds:

These considerations cannot be extended across worlds, because you can change anything to anything by easy stages through some connecting series of possible worlds. The devastating difference is that the series of momentary cross-sections of our real world is uniquely imposed on us, for better or for worse, whereas all manner of paths of continuous gradation from one possible world to another are free for the thinking up. (Quine [1976a], p. 127)

At this point, however, Quine has to face the following dilemma: either the difference between identification of individuals across moments of time and identification of individuals across possible worlds is 'devastating' or it is not.

If the difference is devastating, then the target of Quine's objections is no longer QM in general but only a limited part of it, i.e. metaphysical modal logic dealing with the operators 'necessarily' and 'possibly'. Should a quantified temporal logic operating with 'It will be the case that', 'It was the case that' be constructed, it would be immune to Quine's criticism related to essentialism.

Consider the following pair of sentences in which S is the abbreviation of the temporal monadic operator 'It will soon be the case that' which I borrow from Kaplan ("Opacity" [forthcoming]):

$(\exists x)(x$ is a child $\& \ S(x$ is female$))$

$S(\exists x)(x$ is a child $\& \ x$ is female$)$

The first sentence describes an astonishing event: a male, or an asexual child, will turn into a female. The second sentence describes a very common future event: a human female will be born.

To make sense of the *de re* use, all we need, according to Quine, is the ability to identify individuals across moments of time, a feat which Quine himself concedes that we can perform without appealing to *arbitrary criteria* such as those we have to use for identification across possible worlds. Interpreting *de dicto* usage requires still less. It requires the ability to associate truth-values with moments of time.

Hence it is clear that Quine's revised criticism has a *more limited scope*: it leaves temporal quantified modal logic unaffected if the difference between identification of individuals across moments of time significantly differs from identification of individuals across possible worlds (This was the first horn of the dilemma).

When I say that temporal logic is not plagued by the same difficulties as modal logic, I mean *linear temporal logic*. I concede that the semantics of *branching temporal logic* is hardly better off than possible world semantics insofar as it requires *possible* futures, which raises many of the problems.

Let us now consider the second horn of the dilemma and see how Quine's argument fares if the difference between the two sorts of *identification* is seen as negligible. By this, I do not mean to imply that the difference between the two sorts of *changes* is held to be negligible.

It is unquestionable that changes in the universe which are associated with the passing of time crucially differ from the alterations of the picture of our world which we think up when we freely invent counterfactual situations. But from this striking difference it *does not follow* that the principles of identification across possible worlds are fundamentally different from those which serve to identify individuals across moments of time. If the identification principles are riveted to words of a certain category one could argue that they do double duty, i.e., that they secure both *transworld* as well as *transtime* identification, since words retain their ordinary meaning in science fiction as much as in historical novels, unless they are explicitly redefined.

A. Gupta seems to take advantage of this *linguistic stability* when he says that common nouns (as opposed to predicates) embody principles of identification which "trace *particulars* – a particular man, or bicycle, or, whatever – through worlds (and times)" (A. Gupta [1980], p. 102). For instance, to borrow Gupta's example, two sortals 'persons' and 'passengers' involve different principles of counting – and this explains why if an Airline company has served n passengers during a certain period, we cannot validly infer that it has served n persons during the same time.

Quine claims that essence is *necessary* to identify an object from one possible world to another. But here again his statement badly needs supporting arguments. There might be ways of identifying objects across possible worlds which are less metaphysically loaded. We have mentioned Gupta's appeal to principles of identity ingrained in common nouns, but there are also other solutions such as those which appeal to demonstratives.

Clearly, individual essences are *not sufficient* to identify objects across possible worlds as Salmon showed by this argument:

Let us consider four worlds, W_1, W_2, W_3 and W_4 and two boats a and b, the first of which belongs in W_1 and W_3, the second in W_2 and W_4. Both boats have the same structure and the same number of planks, and an arbitrary threshold is fixed of changes that a boat can undergo without losing its identity. Suppose, for instance, that the threshold stipulates the replacement of at most two planks. In such conditions, one can imagine that, to start with, a is in W_1, and b in W_2, and that they differ by three planks. Suppose that two of a's planks are changed in W_3, so that on our convention a preserves its identity. And suppose that b has one of its planks changed, and is moved to W_4 preserving its identity. It is easy to see that a in W_3 and b in W_4 could have the same composition in that "these two ships do not differ in any way qualitatively or structurally".

From this Salmon concludes that "they differ in their haecceities: the first ship is *this* ship, the second is *that* ship, they are different ships, and that is all there is to it". (Ocuzoglu Salmon [1979], p. 723)

Salmon's thought experiment seems to me to convincingly establish that we can distinguish *this* boat from *that* boat across possible worlds even though the two boats share the same essence. (They are qualitatively and structurally indiscernible.)

To disprove Quine's claim that identification of individuals across possible worlds requires the postulation of individual essences, however, one should take a step further and show not only that essences are not sufficient – as Salmon does – but also that they are not necessary. This step has been taken by Kaplan. Reviving Duns Scotus' concept of *haecceities* Kaplan offers a non-essentialist account of identification. He dubs his doctrine 'haecceitism':

The doctrine that holds that it does make sense to ask – without reference to common attributes and behavior – whether *this* is the same individual in another possible world, that individuals can be extended in logical space (i.e., through possible worlds) in much the way we commonly regard them as being extended in physical space and time, and that a common "thisness" may underlie extreme dissimilarity or distinct thisnesses may underlie great resemblance, I call *Haecceitism*. (Kaplan [1975], p. 217)

Haecceitism based as it is on indexicals should be positively repellent for Quine who cannot even bear proper names and wants to explain them away by definite description which will, in turn, be eliminated à la Russell, but this is not a sufficient reason to dismiss it. Contrary to Aristotelian essentialism, which is a questionable metaphysical doctrine, haecceitism seems to be nothing more than an innocuous semantic theory dealing with the use of demonstratives.

6. Propositional Attitudes[1]

In his 1956 paper "Quantifiers and Propositional Attitudes" Quine observes that-clauses which are introduced by verbs such as 'believes that' or 'desires that' are opaque contexts: co-referential terms cannot be substituted *salva veritate* in these contexts.

From

(28) Ralph believes that the man in the brown hat is a spy

and

(29) The man in the brown hat = the man seen at the beach

it does not follow that

(30) Ralph believes that the man seen at the beach is a spy.

From this, Quine infers that quantification inside these contexts should be rejected as meaningless. But this is counter-intuitive. Surely the candid speaker recognizes a difference in meaning between:

(31) There are people whom Ralph believes are spies

and

(32) Ralph believes that there are spies.

In the first situation Ralph would do well to inform the police. Not so in the second.

Kaplan claims that Quine's inference is faulty. On Kaplan's reconstruction of that inference, Quine takes for granted that 'if an occurrence of a singular term in a formula is purely designative, then the truth value of the formula depends only on *what* the occurrence designates, not on *how* it designates'. From that he concludes that 'if α and β designate the same thing but $\Phi\alpha$ and $\Phi\beta$ differ in truth value, then the indicated occurrence of α in Φ

---

[1] On this topic see T. Burge [1978] and Butrick [1982].

and of β in Φ are not purely designative. But this, Kaplan says, does not follow. "All that follows from (the first statement) is that at least one of the two occurrences is not purely designative" (Kaplan, "Opacity" [forthcoming]).

Hence the irreferential occurrence of constant terms does not at all establish the meaninglessness of quantifying in. Quine, who thinks it does, tries to salvage quantification *de re* and to account for the *de re – de dicto* contrast by postulating a *lexical* ambiguity. The verb 'believes' would not be the same in both sentences. In the *de dicto* sentence (32), the verb 'believes' should be construed as a two-place predicate

(33) x believes-true Y[1]

In the *de re* sentence (31), the same verb should be construed as a three-place predicate

(34) x believes of y that-it-satisfies Z[2]

For instance:

(35) $(\exists y)$ (Ralph believes 'spy' of y)

The *de dicto-de re* contrast also applies to belief-sentences involving a name rather than a bound variable in the clause introduced by 'believes'. Hence we have the *de dicto* statement

(36) Ralph believes 'Ortcutt is a spy',

and the *de re* statement,

(37) Ralph believes 'spy' of Ortcutt.

In (37), the name 'Ortcutt' occurs in a referentially transparent position. Hence the law of existential generalization $Fa \vdash (\forall x) Fx$ applies without any problem. In (36), on the contrary, 'Ortcutt' occurs in a quotation, hence

---

[1] Y is a metalinguistic variable which takes sentences as values and names of sentences as substituents.
[2] Z is a metalinguistic variable which takes predicates as values and names of predicates as substituents.

the law of existential generalization does not apply. At least, it would not apply unless we were allowed to shift the name 'Ortcutt' from the opaque context to a transparent one. Let us call this shift 'exportation'.

Under which condition, is such exportation permitted? Quine answers that it is permitted if the following additional premiss is true:

(38) $(\exists x)$ Ralph believes $(x = \text{Ortcutt})$,

which is the formal rendering of the quasi colloquial expression built on the pattern of the colloquial expression 'knows who a is'

(39) Ralph believes who Ortcutt is.

Quine stresses the similarity between (38) and the additional premiss which Føllesdal proved to be needed for making a term recurring in alethic modal contexts accessible to existential generalization, i.e. the premiss

(40) $(\exists x)$ $\square$ $(x = a)$

Borrowing terms from Kripke and Carnap respectively, Quine describes the situation as follows. Substitutivity of identity and laws of quantification can safely be applied to a term a in modal context if this term is a *rigid* designator, i.e., if (40) holds. The same laws and, moreover, exportation, can safely be applied to a term a in doxastic context if this term is a *vivid* designator.

Quine credits Hintikka with the discovery of this extra premiss required by doxastic logic. But this imputation, as Kvart pointed out is misleading since Hintikka would interpret '$(\exists x)$ $B_s(x=a)$' as 'a exists in all worlds compatible with the beliefs of s', but Hintikka's values of variables in doxastic contexts can be possible individuals unlike Quine's:

... for Hintikka, unlike Quine, the quantification in $[(\exists x)$ $B_s(x=a)]$ need not range over actual individuals, since the actual world need not be among the possible worlds compatible with S's beliefs. But, for Quine, the quantification in $[(\exists x) B_s(x=a)]$ should be interpreted standardly, since it is taken as the requisite condition for exportation ... (Kvart [1982], p. 303 footnote)

I will not dwell on the question whether the premiss Quine appeals to suffices to make exportation valid – Kvart[1] claims it does not – but rather discuss Quine's sustained comparison between propositional attitudes and modalities.

Quine claims that *de re* propositional attitudes are not better off than *de re* modalities. They suffer from the same shortcomings:

The notion of knowing or believing who or what someone or something is, is utterly dependent on context. Sometimes, when we ask who someone is, we see the face and want the name; sometimes the reverse. Sometimes we want to know his role in the community. Of itself the notion is empty.

It and the notion of essence are on a par. Both make sense in context. Relative to a particular inquiry, some predicates may play a more basic role than others ... and these may be treated as essential. (Quine [1977b], p. 121)

The moral to be drawn is that the notion of vivid designator should be abandoned just as much as the notion of essentialism. But if we do so the *de re-de dicto* contrast collapses. The distinction between merely believing that there are spies and suspecting a specific person goes by the board. Quine, however, is ready to go that far

At first this seems intolerable, but it grows on one. I now think the distinction is every bit as empty, apart from context, as that of vivid designator ... (Quine [1977b], p. 121)

There are unquestionably *de re* and *de dicto* sentences which can be interpreted either way, depending on the context. For instance, the *de dicto* sentence (41) addressed to Bill by John when Bill has just trodden on John's feet is intended as a *de re* and will miss the mark if Bill does not read this *de dicto* sentence as a *de re* statement in which he is the *res* [thing] referred to.

(41) There are people who really do not worry. (Ducrot [1980], p. 14)

But contrary to Quine, I contend that for certain *syntactic* categories of sentences, the *de dicto – de re* distinction is vital and can hardly be weakened by the *context*. The *syntactic category* of imperatives is a case in point.

---

[1] Kvart offers a counter-example and then provides an alternative requirement for exportation: "... when one is given a premise of the form '*s* believes '*Fa*'', one may export to the conclusion '*s* believes '*F*' of *a*' provided the intended reference of '*a*' by *s* (in that belief) coincides with the *denotation* of '*a*', that is with *a*". (Kvart [1982], p. 304)

Imperatives render the *de re – de dicto* distinction *dramatically* important as can be seen from the following example: If an executioner has been instructed to kill Ortcutt, sentenced to death, he can infer the *de re* imperative

(42) Of someone, kill him!

but certainly *not* the *de dicto* imperative:

(43) Kill someone!

7. What is Left After the Elimination of the *de re* Construction?

De dicto constructions, i.e., the second grade of modal involvement, can always be eliminated by a metalinguistic ascent, i.e., by a retreat to the first grade of modal involvement.

(44) It is necessary that $9 > 7$

will be rewritten

(45) '$9 > 7$' is analytic

and, similarly,

(46) Ptolemeus believed that the earth is still

will be rewritten

(47) Ptolemeus believed 'the earth is still'.

The *de dicto* attitudes seen as dyadic relations[1] between people or other animals and sentences are more important for Quine than the statements predicating analyticity since it is one of his main contentions that the synthetic-analytic dichotomy is spurious.

---

[1] These relations should not be understood as implying that Ptolemeus spoke English.

By reducing *de re* propositional attitudes and *de re* modalities to *de dicto* constructions, Quine reaches the conclusion that only two sorts of constructions remain: (1) constructions which are referentially transparent and (2) quotation contexts which are referentially opaque. One could even say that only one construction remains since quotation can be explained away. Extensionalism occupies the whole scene; intensionality has vanished in the air.

Recently, however, Barwise and Perry have pointed out that there are after all constructions which are stubbornly *de re*, and yet intensional, i.e., the constructions made out of verbs of perception, combined with 'naked infinitives', i.e. infinitives not introduced by 'to'.

To illustrate Barwise's and Perry's point, let us take the following sentence which Quine examines in "Reference and Modality"

(48) Crassus heard Tully denounce Catiline

Clearly the three names occur in *transparent position* and existential generalization applies to all of them straightforwardly. Yet the verb 'heard' + naked infinitive generates a hyper-intensional context since the conjunction of a tautological naked infinitive to the initial naked infinitive can turn a true sentence into a falsehood, as is the case in (49):

(49) Crassus heard Tully denounce Catiline and Lucrezia Borgia cough or not cough.

The sentence (49) is false. Crassus cannot have heard Lucrezia Borgia at all since he died several centuries before Lucrezia Borgia was born. To account for the inference potential of this type of constructions, Barwise and Perry developed a situation semantics. This is not the place to assess the value of this new brand of model theoretic semantics. All I want to do here is see how Quine would tackle the problem.

Commenting on sentence (48), Quine writes:

This statement affirms a relation between three persons, and the persons remain so related independently of the names applied to them. (Quine [1953d], p. 142)

In other words, Quine lumps together 'heard' and 'denounce'.

Admittedly Quine could explain the falsity of (49). He could say that (49) has the following form where F stands for 'heard denounce' G stands for 'heard cough or not cough' and 'a', 'b', 'c', 'd' stand for 'Crassus', 'Tully', 'Cataline' and 'Borgia' respectively.

(50) $F(a, b, c) \& G(a, d)$

Unfortunately, this ruthless regimentation which runs counter to the principle of compositionality by treating heard + infinitive as a unit will make it impossible to account for the fact that (48) entails

(51) Crassus heard something,

or that tautological naked infinitives can be introduced under certain conditions. For instance (52) can be added to (48)

(52) and Tully cough or not cough

without altering the truth value of the resulting compound.

It would be unfair to quarrel with Quine on his relational reading of 'heard denounce'. Quine is interested in devising a canonical notation which reflects the important features of the world and *not* in the scientific study of the logic of natural language as such. He makes this clear in "Methodological reflections on current linguistic theory" in a comment on the philosophical significance of tense logic:

A logic of tense is a towering triviality which we have no excuse to put up with if our concern is merely with the scientific use of language rather than with the scientific study of it. (Quine [1970d], p. 453)

This sweeping generalization is, however, an over-simplification and an exaggeration. (See J.L. van Benthem, *The Logic of Time* [1983]). Can we accommodate science in an extensionalist canonical notation? Vuillemin argued that we can accommodate mechanics (see his report on Dagfinn Føllesdal's paper "Quantified modal logic and essentialism") in this framework. In "Philosophical Perspectives on Quantification in Tense and Modal Logic" however, N. Cocchiarella [1984] presents statements of the special relativity physics whose formal rendering requires a logic containing both modal and tense operators. The question whether we can also accommodate other natural sciences is an open one. Quine should be credited with the merit of having raised this question.

Conclusion

In Chapter I, I began by considering "Two Dogmas of Empiricism", and argued that the dogmas in question are not at root identical. I discussed Benjamin Cohen's claim that the alleged analytical statements are hidden typicality statements. I defended the analytic-synthetic distinction and examined Priest's defence of the distinction between logical truths and factual truths. I then surveyed the various versions of holism Quine has put forward and argued that some of them collapse holism into conventionalism. However, Dummett's claim that Quine has to give up either holism or empiricism was rejected, on the ground, amongst others, that it overlooks Quine's conception of an observation-occasion sentence as an *unstructured* whole. Chomsky, on the other hand, has criticized Quine for neglecting a distinction which few are prepared to abandon easily, namely that between language and theory. I defended a weaker position which is also consistent with the rejection of the analytic-synthetic distinction: language and theory are not identical but they are inseparable.

In Chapter II, Quine's behavioural semantics was compared with platonistic and mentalistic semantics. The thesis that translation is indeterminate was examined in detail, and related to field work on translation. I developed arguments both against that thesis and against its corollary, the thesis that reference is inscrutable. Developing a suggestion due to Moravcsik, and taking advantage of Holdcroft's recent work on the subject, I argued that indeterminacy and inscrutability can be reduced to a phenomenon of very limited importance if the constraints of language learning are brought to bear on the issue.

In Chapter III, the criterion of ontological commitment was examined closely. I discussed Vuillemin's objection at length, and offered a vindication of Quine's criterion which displays the connection between his criterion and Tarski's semantics. I discussed Trapp's claim that Quine's criterion deals with *extensive* ontology only (as opposed to *intensive* ontology), and ignored ontological distinctions drawn by Conceptualists and Moderate Realists. Can we promote philosophical ontology to the status of a science whose categories differ in degree but not in kind from those of more mundane sciences? Can we consistently hold that ontology is relative and that truth is not relative? Quine's work raises these questions in a sharp form. He himself argues that both questions have an affirmative answer, and I argued that he is right to do so. Truth can remain invariant, even though ontology changes. However, Quine also claims that truth is internal to theories. How can we reconcile the absoluteness of truth with its immanence to theories?

In Chapter IV, I discussed that problem. In the same chapter I showed that Quine has superseded the distinction between transcendent and immanent questions by absorbing the former into the latter. This radicalization, I described as a crucial move in the *Positivismus Streit*. Quine's epistemology has been criticized for being too naturalistic and not normative enough. I showed that these objections are misguided. Like any brand of empiricism, Quine's empiricism contains a normative ingredient. This ingredient is not threatened by the immanence of truth: truth is immanent to theory, but empirical evidence remains transcendent to theory. All theoretical statements have to face the tribunal of experience. A more serious threat arises in connection with another of Quine's challenging views: his claim that scientific theories are underdetermined by observational data. I argued that, as soon as the latter thesis is combined with the claim that truth is immanent to theories, relativism follows. After defending the Underdetermination Thesis against those who contend that it involves an implicit appeal to the traditional notion of meaning, I nevertheless suggested that we should abandon it as ill-founded. I also argued against the expedient which Quine uses to dodge relativism.

Chapter V is devoted to a problem which Quine tackled, I think successfully, the problem of the demarcation of logic. The most frequently invoked definition of a logical truth rests on an arbitrary decision as to what counts as a logical constant. Here we owe an important innovation to Quine, namely, a definition of logic which does not rest on the distinction usually invoked between logical and non-logical terms, but on the distinction (admittedly language-relative) between lexicon and grammar. I also considered the controversy between Quine and Strawson, about the allegedly intensional nature of the notion of logical truth and discussed an objection made by Hinman, Kim and Stich. The chapter ended with a comparison between Quine's semantic demarcation of logic and Hacking's proof-theoretic demarcation.

Chapter VI deals with deviant logic. Can the laws of logic be changed without changing the senses of the logical constants that they contain?

What is at issue here is the very possibility of alternative logics; but Quine has clearly vacillated a great deal in the answers he has given to this crucial question. In my view, his most recent position, which allows for revisability, is a step in the right direction, even though too timid a step.

The final chapter (VII) tries to assess the outcome of the war of attrition that Quine has waged for more than thirty years against quantified modal logic. A great deal of attention is given to an argument which Quine spelt out against quantified modal logic (the so-called 'slingshot argument' to borrow Barwise's and Perry's terminology). The conclusion of this argument is that modal logic is either referentially opaque or non modal. In his unpublished doctoral dissertation, Føllesdal found a way to escape this calamitous dilemma. He showed that referential transparency is compatible with intensionality. There is, however, a price to pay. As Quine expected, we have to endorse essentialism. Yet the commitment to essentialism which is needed was proved by Ruth Barcan Marcus and Terence Parsons to be rather harmless: only the meaningfulness of essentialism, not its truth, has to be assumed. Why then has not Kripke's and others' construction of a rigorous semantics put an end to Quine's attack against quantified modal logic? The answer can be found in Quine's belief that the very notion of identification across possible worlds is saddled with essentialism. I argued against this claim and showed how the question of identification can be separated from the problem of essentialism. Hintikka's, Kaplan's and Gupta's findings have been used here. I ended up by discussing perceptual reports. I contended that Quine's extensionalistic framework cannot accommodate them, and that it is doubtful that it can succeed as a universal notation, however appealing it may be. Yet it can accommodate mathematics and this is a result of momentous importance which Quine contributed to establish when he showed how one can eliminate the hidden appeal to properties which he has uncovered in *Principia Mathematica*.

Bibliography

Apostel, L.	1974	*Matière et Forme*, vol. I, Ghent: Editions Communication and Cognition.
Ayer, A.J.	1956	*The Problem of Knowledge*, London: Pelican.
Barcan Marcus, R.,	1947	"The modal functional Calculus of the first order", *Journal of Symbolic Logic*, 11, pp. 1–16.
	1967	"Essentialism in Modal Logic", *Noûs*, 1, pp. 91–96.
Barwise, J.	1981	"Scenes and Other Situations", *The Journal of Philosophy*, LXXVIII, pp. 369–397.
Barwise, J., and Perry, J.	1981a	"Semantic Innocence and Uncompromising Situations", *Midwest Studies in Philosophy*, VI, (The Foundations of Analytic Philosophy), pp. 387–403.
	1981b	"Situations and Attitudes", *The Journal of Philosophy*, LXXVIII, pp. 668–691.
Bayart, A.	1958	"La correction de la logique modale du premier et second ordre S 5", *Logique et Analyse*, 1, pp. 28–45
Berger, A.	1980	"Quine on 'Alternative Logics' and Verdict Tables", *Journal of Philosophy* 77, pp. 259–277
Bergström, L.	1984	"Undetermination and Realism", *Erkenntnis* 21, pp. 349–365.
Berka, K.	1983	"Logic with or without Ontology: a Marxist Approach", *Teorie Rozvoje Vědy*, VII/4, pp. 1–19.

Bocheński, J.M., et al.,	1956	*The Problem of Universals*, Notre-Dame: University of Notre Dame Press.
Bondi, H.	²1960	*Cosmology*, Cambridge U.P.
Bonevac, D.A.	1980	*Ontological Reduction and Abstract Entities*, Ph.D. dissertation: Univ. of Pittsburg, Univ. Microfilms International.
Burdick, H.	1982	"A logical form for the propositional Attitudes", *Synthese*, 52, no. 2, pp. 185–230.
Burge, T.	1978	"Belief and Synonymy", *Journal of Philosophy*, LXXV, pp. 119–138.
Burkhardt, H.	1980	*Logik und Semiotik in der Philosophie von Leibniz*, Munich: Philosophia Verlag.
Callaway, H.G.	1982	"Semantic Theory and Language: A Perspective", *Proceedings of the South Western Philosophical Society*, Supplement to *Philosophical Topics*, Denver, 1982, pp. 61–70.
	1985	"Meaning without Analyticity", *Logique et Analyse*, pp. 41–60.
Carnap, R.	1936	"Testability and Meaning", *Philosophy of Science*, vol. 3, 1936, pp. 419–471; vol. 4, 1937, pp. 1–40.
	1937	*The Logical Syntax of Language*, trans. Smeaton, London: Routledge and Kegan (2nd ed. 1964, first German language edition: *Die logische Syntax der Sprache*, 1934).
	1950	"Empiricism, Semantics and Ontology", *Revue Internationale de Philosophie*, repr. in: *Meaning and Necessity*, Chicago: Phoenix Books, ²1956.
	²1956	*Meaning and Necessity*, Chicago: Phoenix Books, Supplement, pp. 222–229.
	1966	*Philosophical Foundations of Physics*, Basic Books.

Chateaubriand	1973	quoted in Chihara, Ch.S., *Ontology and the Vicious Circle Principle*, Ithaca: Cornell University Press.
Chihara, Ch.S.	1973	*Ontology and the Vicious Circle Principle*, Ithaca: Cornell University Press.
Chomsky, N.	1957	*Syntactic Structures*, The Hague: Mouton.
	1968	"Quine's Empirical Assumptions", *Synthese*, vol. 19, 1968–1969, no. 1/2, Dec., pp. 53–68.
Church, A.	1958	"Ontological Commitment", *Journal of Philosophy*, LV, pp. 1008–1014.
Clavelin, M.	1983	"Quine contre Carnap, la polémique sur l'analyticité et sa portée", *Revue Internationale de Philosophie*, 144–145, pp. 69–92.
Cocchiarella, N.	1980	"Sortals, Natural Kinds and Re-Identification", in L. Aqvist and F. Guenthner, *Tense Logic*, Logique et Analyse, 80, pp. 85–120.
	1984	"Philosophical Perspectives on Quantification in Tense and Modal Logic", in *Handbook of Philosophical Logic*, vol. II, *Extensions of Classical Logics*, ed. by D. Gabbay and F. Guenthner, Dordrecht: Reidel, pp. 309–353.
Cohen, B.	1982	*Understanding Natural Kinds*, Ph.D. dissertation: Stanford University, Stanford, CA.
Craig, W.	1956	"Replacement of Auxiliary Expressions", *The Philosophical Review*, LXV, pp. 38–55.
Dalla Chiara, M.L.	1984	"The Relevance of Quantum Logic", *International Congress for Logic, Methodology and the Philosophy of Science*, Salzburg, forthcoming, North-Holland.

Davidson, D.	1974	"On the very idea of a conceptual scheme", *Proceedings and Addresses of the American Philosophical Association* (47), reprinted in: *Truth and Interpretation*, Oxford: Clarendon Press, pp. 183–198.
Deckert, M.	1973	"Quine, Strawson and Logical Truth", *Philosophical Studies* 24, pp. 54–56 (quoted in P. Hinman, J. Kim, S. Stich).
Degen, J.W.	1983	*Systeme der kumulativen Logik*, Munich: Philosophia Verlag.
Destouches-Fevrier, P.	1951	*La structure des théories physiques*, Paris: Presses Universitaires de France.
Dewey, J.	1925	*Experience and Nature*, La Salle: Open Court.
Dilworth, C.	1981	*Scientific Progress*, Dordrecht: Reidel.
Ducrot, O.	1980	*Les mots du Discours*, Paris: Editions de Minuit.
Duhem, P.	1906	*La théorie physique son objet et sa structure*, (^{2}1914: with new appendix), Paris: Rivières.
Dummett, M.	1973	*Frege, Philosophy of Language*, London: Duckworth (^{2}1981).
Føllesdal, D.	1961	*Referential Opacity*, Ph.D. dissertation: Harvard University.
	1967	"Knowledge, Identity and Existence", *Theoria* 33, pp. 1–27.
	1973	"Indeterminacy of Translation and Underdetermination of the Theory of Nature", *Dialectica* 27, pp. 289–301.
	–	"Quantified Modal Logic and Essentialism" (forthcoming).
Frege, G.	1918 –1919	"The Thought: a Logical Inquiry", trans. by A. and M. Quinton, *Mind* vol. 65, 1956, pp. 289–311; reprinted in: *Philosophical Logic*, ed. by P.F. Strawson, Oxford: Oxford University Press, 1967.

Friedman, M.	1975	"Physicalism and the Indeterminacy of Translation", *Noûs* 19, pp. 353–374.
Geach, P.T.	1965	"Some Problems about Time", *Proceedings of the British Academy*, Cambridge University Press, pp. 321–336.
Gibson, R.F.	1982	*The Philosophy of W.V. Quine*, Tampa: University of South Florida.
Glotzbach, Ph.A.	1979	*Behavior, Meaning and Reference in the Philosophy of Quine*, Ph.D. dissertation: Yale University.
Gochet, P.	1980	*Outline of a Nominalist Theory of Propositions*, Dordrecht: Reidel.
Gottlieb, D.	1980	*Ontological Economy*, Oxford: Clarendon Press.
Grice, H.P. Strawson, P.F.	1956	"In Defence of a Dogma", *The Philosophical Review* LXV, no. 2, pp. 141–58 repr. in: *Readings in the Philosophy of Language*, ed. by J.F. Rosenberg and Ch. Travis, Englewood Cliffs: Prentice Hall, pp. 81–94.
Grünbaum, A.	1960	"The Duhemian Argument", *Philosophical Review* repr. in S. Harding, *Can Theories be Refuted?* Dordrecht: Reidel (1970), pp. 116–131.
Gupta, A.	1980	*The Logic of Common Nouns*, Yale University Press.
Haack, R.	1978	"Quine's Theory of Logic", *Erkenntnis* 13, pp. 231–259.
Haack, S.	1974	*Deviant Logic*, Cambridge: Cambridge University Press.
	1977	"Analyticity and Logical Truth in 'The Roots of Reference'", *Theoria* 43, pp. 129–143.
	1978	*Philosophy of Logics*, Cambridge: Cambridge University Press.
Hacking, I.	1979	"What is Logic"?, *Journal of Philosophy*, LXXVI, pp. 285–319.
Haller, R.	1982	*Urteile und Ereignisse*, Freiburg – München: Karl Alber.

Harding, S.	1970	*Can Theories be Refuted?*, Dordrecht: Reidel.
Harrison, B.	1980	*Introduction to the Philosophy of Language*, London: Methuen.
Hauptli, B.	1983	"Quine's Theorizing about Theories", *Synthese*, vol. 57, no. 1, Oct. pp. 21–33.
Hesse, M.	1976	"Duhem, Quine and a New Empiricism", The Royal Institute of Philosophy Lectures, reprinted in: S. Harding, *Can Theories be Refuted?*, Dordrecht: Reidel (1970), pp. 184–204.
Hickman, L.	1980	*Modern Theories of Higher Level Predicates*, Munich: Philosophia Verlag.
Higginbotham,	1983	"The Logic of Perceptual Reports: an Extensional Alternative to Situation Semantics", *The Journal of Philosophy*, LXXX, pp. 100–127.
Hinman, P., Kim, J., Stich, S.	1968	"Logical Truth Revisited", *Journal of Philosophy* LXV, pp. 495–500.
Hintikka, J.	1961	"Modality and Quantification", *Theoria*, vol. 27, pp. 110–128.
	1967	"Individuals, Possible Worlds, and Epistemic Logic", *Noûs*, vol. 1, pp. 33–62.
	1968	"Behavioural Criteria of Radical Translation", *Synthese* 19, no. 1/2, pp. 69–81.
Holdcroft, D.	1985	"Propositions, Indeterminacy and Holism" in: *Exercises in Analysis*, ed. by I. Hacking, Cambridge: Cambridge University Press, pp. 125–145.
Jonathan Cohen, L.	²1966	*The Diversity of Meaning*, London: Methuen.
Kanger, St.	1957	*Provability in Logic*, Stockholm: Almqvist and Wiksell.

Kaplan, D.	1975	"How to Russell a Frege-Church", *The Journal of Philosophy*, LXXII, pp. 716–729, repr. in M.J. Loux, ed., *The Possible and the Actual*, Ithaca: Cornell Univ. Press (1979) pp. 210–224.
		"Opacity", forthcoming in: *The Philosophy of Quine*, the Library of Living Philosophers, La Salle: Open Court.
Katz, J.J.	1972	*Semantic Theory*, New York: Harper and Row.
	1975	"Recent Criticisms of Intensionalism" in: K. Gunderson, ed., *Language, Mind and Knowledge*, University of Minnesota Press, pp. 36–130.
Keenan, Ed.L., and Faltz, L.M.	1984	*Boolean Semantics for Natural Language*, Dordrecht: Reidel.
Kim, J.	1968	see: Hinman, P.
Kripke, S.	1959	"A Completeness Theorem in Modal Logic", *The Journal of Symbolic Logic*, vol. 24, pp. 1–14.
	1963	"Semantical Considerations on Modal Logic", *Acta Philosophica Fennica*, XVI, pp. 83–94; repr. in: Linsky, *Reference and Modality*, Oxford Readings in Philosophy (1971), pp. 63–72.
Kalinowski, G.	1984	*Sémiotique et Philosophie*, Amsterdam – Paris: Benjamins.
Küng, G.	1967	*Ontology and the Logistic Analysis of Language*, Dordrecht: Reidel (revised version of *Ontologie und logistische Analyse der Sprache*, Wien: Springer, 1963).
Kvart, I.	1982	"Quine and Modalities *De Re*: A Way Out", *The Journal of Philosophy*, LXXIX, 1982, pp. 295–328.
Ladmiral, J.R.	1979	*Traduire, théorèmes pour la traduction*, Paris: Payot.

Langford, C.H.	1932	see: Lewis, C.I.
Lauener, H.	1982	*Willard V.O. Quine*, Munich: C.H. Beck.
Lautman, A.	1977	*Essai sur l'unité des mathématiques et divers écrits*, Paris: Union Générale d'Editions.
Leibniz, G.W.		*Opuscules et fragments inédits de Leibniz*, Edited by Couturat, Paris, 1903, Hildesheim: 1961.
Lenin, V.I.	1983	*Collected Works*, vol. 38, Moscow (1961), quoted by Berka, K., "Logic with or without Ontology: a Marxist Approach".
Levy, M.	1979	"Relations entre chimie et physique", *Epistemologia*, vol. 2, pp. 337–369.
Lewis, C.I., and Langford, C.H.	1932	*Symbolic Logic*, New York – Dover: ²1959.
McRobbie, M.A.	1979	*A Proof Theoretic Investigation of Relevant and Modal Logics*, Ph.D. dissertation: Australian National University, Canberra.
Marcus, Ruth Barcan,	1947	see: Barcan Marcus, R.
Moore, G.E.	1919–20	"External and Internal Relations", *Proceedings of the Aristotelian Society*, reprinted in: *Philosophical Studies* (1922), London: Routledge and Kegan Paul, pp. 276–309.
Moravcsik, J.	1975	*Understanding Language*, The Hague: Mouton.
Mulligan, K., Simons, P., Smith B.	1984	"Truth-Makers", *Philosophy and Phenomenological Research*, XLIV, 3, pp. 287–321.
Newton-Smith, W.H.	1978	"The Underdetermination of Theories by data", *Proceedings of the Aristotelian Society*, Supplementary vol. 52, pp. 71–91.
	1981	*The Rationality of Science*, London: Routledge & Kegan Paul.

Orenstein, A.	1984	"Referential and Non-referential Substitutional Quantifiers", *Synthese* 60, pp. 145–157.
Oppenheimer, R.	1962	"Réflexions sur la science et la culture", in *Recherches et débats du Centre catholique des Intellectuels français*, Cahier 39, pp. 108–112.
Parsons, Ch.	1971	"A Plea for Substitutional Quantification", *Journal of Philosophy* LXVIII, pp. 231–237.
Parsons, T.	1969	"Essentialism and Quantified Modal Logic", *The Philosophical Review*, LXXVIII, pp. 35–52, repr. in Linsky, *Reference and Modality*, Oxford Readings in Philosophy (1971), pp. 73–87.
Pascal, B.	1914	"De l'art de persuader", *Oeuvres*, tome IX, Paris: Hachette.
Peacocke, C.	1978	"With Reference to the Roots", *Inquiry* 21, 1, pp. 105–129.
Popper, K.	1959	*The Logic of Scientific Discovery*, London: Hutchinson.
	1963	*Conjectures and Refutations: The Growth of Scientific Knowledge*, London: Routledge and Kegan Paul.
Priest, G.	1979	"Two Dogmas of Quineanism", *The Philosophical Quarterly*, vol. 29, pp. 289–301.
Putnam, H.	1982	"Why Reason Can't be Naturalized", *Synthese*, vol. 52, no. 1, July.
Quine, W.V.O.	1936	"Truth by Convention", in: *Philosophical Essays for Alfred North Whitehead*, repr. in: *The Ways of Paradox*, New York: Random House (^{2}1976), pp. 77–106.
	1937	"New Foundations for Mathematical Logic", *American Mathematical Monthly*, repr. in: *From a Logical Point of View*, Cambridge, Mass. 1953 (^{2}1961), pp. 80–101.

1939a "A Logistical Approach to the Ontological Problem", repr. in: *The Ways of Paradox* (^{2}1976), pp. 197–202.

1939b "Designation and Existence", *The Journal of Philosophy*, XXXVI, pp. 701–709, repr. in: H. Feigl and W. Sellars, eds., *Readings in Philosophical Analysis*, New York: Appelton Century Crofts 1949, pp. 44–51.

1940 *Mathematical Logic*, Cambridge, Mass.: Harvard University Press.

1943 "Notes on Existence and Necessity", *Journal of Philosophy*, XL, pp. 113–127.

1947 "On Universals", *The Journal of Symbolic Logic*, 12, pp. 43–48.

1948 "On What There Is" repr. in: *From a Logical Point of View*, Cambridge, Mass.: 1953, (^{2}1961), pp. 1–19.

1950 *Methods of Logic*, New York: Holt.

1951a "Two Dogmas of Empiricism", repr. in: *From a Logical Point of View*, Cambridge, Mass.: 1953, (^{2}1961), pp. 20–46.

1951b "On Carnap's Views on Ontology", repr. in: *The Ways of Paradox* (^{2}1976), pp. 203–211.

1953a "Mr. Strawson on Logical Theory", *Mind*, vol. 62, repr. in: *The Ways of Paradox* (^{2}1976), pp. 137–157.

1953b "Three Grades of Modal Involvement", repr. in: *The Ways of Paradox* (^{2}1976), pp. 158–176.

1953c "Logic and the Reification of Universals", Part of that paper came into print as part of "On Universals", *Journal of Symbolic Logic*, 1947, repr. in: *From a Logic Point of View* Cambridge, Mass.: 1953, (^{2}1961), pp. 102–129

1953d	"Reference and Modality", repr. in: *From a Logical Point of View* (fusion of [1943] with "The Problem of Interpreting Modal Logic" [1947]) (^{2}1961), pp. 139–159.
1953e	"Meaning in Linguistics", *From a Logical Point of View* (^{2}1961), pp. 47–64.
1954	"The Scope and Language of Science", repr. in: *The Ways of Paradox* (^{2}1976), pp. 228–245.
1956	"Quantifiers and Propositional Attitudes", repr. in *The Ways of Paradox* (^{2}1976), pp. 185–196.
1960a	*Word and Object*, M.I.T. and New York: Wiley and Sons.
1960b	"Carnap and Logical Truth", repr. in: *The Ways of Paradox* (^{2}1976), pp. 107–132.
1963a	*Set Theory and Its Logic*, Cambridge: The Belknap Press.
1963b	"A Comment on Grünbaum's Claim", *Boston Studies in the Philosophy of Science*, vol. I., ed. by M. Wartowsky, repr. in: *Can Theories be Refuted?*, ed. by S. Harding, 1970, p. 132.
1964	"Ontological Reduction and the World of Numbers", repr. in: *The Ways of Paradox* (^{2}1976), pp. 212–220.
1966	*The Ways of Paradox and other Essays*, New York: Random House (second ed. 1976).
1968a	"Replies (to Smart)" in: *Word and Objection*, Synthese, vol. 19, no. 1/2, 1968.
1968b	"Replies (to Chomsky)", Ibid.
1968c	"Replies (to Hintikka)", Ibid.
1968d	"Replies (to Strawson)", Ibid.

1968e	"Epistemology naturalized", repr. in: *Ontological Relativity*, 1969.
1968f	"Existence and Quantification", *L'Age de la Science*, repr. in: *Ontological Relativity*, 1969, pp. 91–113.
1969	*Ontological Relativity and other Essays*, New York: Columbia University Press.
1970a	"Grades of Theoreticity", *Experience and Theory*, ed. by L. Foster and J.W. Swanson, The University of Massachusetts Press, pp. 1–17.
1970b	"On the Reasons for Indeterminacy of Translation", *The Journal of Philosophy*, LXVII, pp. 178–183.
1970c	*Philosophy of Logic*, Englewood Cliffs: Prentice-Hall.
1970d	"Methodological Reflections on Current Linguistic Theory", repr. in: *Semantics of Natural Language* ed. by D. Davidson and G. Harman, pp. 442–454.
1972	Review of M.K. Munitz, ed., *Identity and Individuation* in: *The Journal of Philosophy*, LXIX, pp. 488–497.
1974	*The Roots of Reference*, La Salle: Open Court.
1975a	"The Nature of Natural Knowledge" in G.E.M. Anscombe et al., *Mind and Language*, Wolfson College Lectures 1974, ed. by S. Guttenplan, Oxford: Clarendon Press, 1975, pp. 67–81.
1975b	"On Empirically Equivalent Systems of the World", *Erkenntnis* 9, pp. 313–328.
1976a	"Worlds away", *The Journal of Philosophy* LXXIII, pp. 859–864, repr. in: *Theories and Things* (1981), pp. 124–128.
1976b	"Whither Physical Objects?", in: *Essays in Memory of Imre Lakatos*, Dordrecht: Reidel, pp. 497–504.

	1977a	"Facts of the Matter" in *American Philosophy: from Edwards to Quine*, ed. by Shahan and Merrill, repr. in: *Essays on the Philosophy of Quine*, ed. by R.S. Shahan, and Ch. Swoyer, Hassocks: The Harvester Press, pp. 155–169.
	1977b	"Intensions Revisited", *Midwest Studies in Philosophy* II, pp. 5–11, repr. in: *Theories and Things* (1981), pp. 113–123.
	1978	"Comments on Newton-Smith", *Analysis* 1979, p. 67.
	1979	"On Not Learning to Quantify", *The Journal of Philosophy* 1979, pp. 429–430.
	1981a	*Theories and Things*, Harvard: Belknap Press.
	1981b	"Reply to Stroud", *Midwest Studies in Philosophy* VI, *The Foundations of Analytic Philosophy*, The University of Minnesota Press, pp. 473–475.
	1982	"Burdick's Attitudes", *Synthese* 52, no. 2, pp. 231–32.
	1983	"Ontology and Ideology Revisited", *The Journal of Philosophy* LXXX, pp. 499–502.
	–	"Meaning, Reference and Truth"; Lecture held in Palermo: 1985 (forthcoming).
Quine, W.V.O., and Ullian, J.S.	1970	*The Web of Belief*, New York: Random House (2nd revised ed. 1978).
Richards, Th.	1979	"How Quine didn't learn to quantify", *The Journal of Philosophy* LXXVI, pp. 421–429.
Ricketts, Th.	1982	"Rationality, Translation and Epistemology Naturalized", *The Journal of Philosophy* LXXIX, pp. 117–136.
Rogers, R.	1963	"A Survey of Formal Semantics", *Synthese* 15, pp. 17–56, reprinted in: *Logic and Philosophy for Linguistics*, ed. by J.M.E. Moravcsik, The Hague: Mouton (1974), pp. 48–82.

Romanos, G.D.	1983	*Quine and Analytic Philosophy*, Cambridge, *The Journal of Philosophy* LXXIX, (1982) M.I.T. Press, 1983.
Russell, B.	1940	*An Inquiry into Meaning and Truth*, London: Allen and Unwin.
Ruytinx, J.	1962	*La problématique philosophique de l'unité de la science*, Bibliothèque de la Faculté de Philosophie et Lettres de l'Université de Liège, Fasc. CLXIV, Paris: Les Belles Lettres.
Ryle, G.	1954	*Dilemmas*, Cambridge: Cambridge Univ. Press.
Salmon, M.O.	1979	"How Not to Derive Essentialism from the Theory of Reference", *The Journal of Philosophy*, vol. LXXVI, pp. 703–725.
Scheffler, I., and Chomsky, N.	1958 –1959	"What is said to be", *Proceedings of the Aristotelian Society*, pp. 71–82.
Scotus		*Reportata Parisiensia* II, d. 12, q. 5, un. 8 and 13.
Simons, P.	1984	see: Mulligan, Simons, and Smith.
Smith, B.	1984	see: Mulligan, Simons, and Smith.
Smith, B., ed.	1982	*Parts and Moments. Studies in Logic and Formal Ontology*, Munich: Philosophia Verlag.
Sosa, E.	1983	"Nature Unmirrored Epistemology Naturalized", *Synthese*, vol. 55, no. 7, pp. 49–72.
Stich, S.	1968	see: Hinman, Kim, and Stich.
Strawson, P.	1956	see: Grice.
	1957	"Propositions, Concepts and Logical Truth", *Philosophical Quarterly* 7, pp. 15–25, repr. in: *Logico-Linguistic Papers*, London: Methuen, 1971, pp. 116–129.
Stroud, B.	1981	"The Significance of Naturalized Epistemology", *Midwest Studies in Philosophy* VI, pp. 455–471.

Tarski, A.	1936	"On the Concept of Logical Consequence", in *Logic, Semantics, Metamathematics*, Oxford: Clarendon Press, 1956, pp. 409–420.
Taylor, B.	1970	*Universals and Predication*, M.A. thesis, University of Melbourne, Parkville.
Thom, P.	1977	"Termini Obliqui and the Logic of Relations", *Archiv für Geschichte der Philosophie* 59, 143–155.
	1982	"Conversion of Propositions containing singular or Quantified Terms in Pseudo-Scotus", *History and Philosophy of Logic* 3, 129–149
Trapp, W.R.	1976	*Analytische Ontologie. Der Begriff der Existenz in Sprache und Logik*, Frankfurt/M.: Vittorio Klostermann.
Ullian, J.S. (with Quine)	1970	*The Web of Belief*, see: Quine.
Van Bendegem, J.P.	1983	*Onderzoek naar de mogelijkheid van een empirische, eindige wiskunde en naar de implikaties ervan voor de relatie wiskunde – werkelijkheid, met bijzondere aandacht voor de getalnotie, de paradoksen van Zeno en de stelling von Gödel*, Ph.D. dissertation, University of Ghent.
Vuillemin, J.	1968	*Lěons sur la première philosophie de Russell*, Paris: A. Colin.
	1971	*La logique et le monde sensible*, Paris: Flammarion.
	1979	"On Duhem's and Quine's Theses", *Grazer Philosophische Studien*, vol. 9, pp. 69–96.
Waragai, T.	1979	"Ontological Burden of Grammatical Categories", *Annals of the Japan Association for Philosophy of Science*, Tokyo, vol. 5, no. 4, March, pp. 185–205.
Weyl, H.	1949	*Philosophy of Mathematics and Science*, Princeton University Press.

Whitehead, A.N., and Russell, B.	1910	*Principia Mathematica*, Cambridge (2nd ed. 1925).
Wilson, Mark	1980	"The Observational Uniqueness of some Theories", *The Journal of Philosophy* LXXVII, pp. 208–233.
Wittgenstein, L.	1922	*Tractatus logico-philosophicus*, German ed. 1918, (1st Engl. trans. 1922, 2nd trans. D.F. Pears and B.F. McGuinness) London: Routledge and Kegan.
Zuber, R.	1978	"Analyticity and Genericness", *Grazer Philosophische Studien* 6, pp. 63–73.

Index of Names

d'Alembert 115
Ammonius 79
Apostel, L. 144
Aristotle 45, 79
Ayer, Sir Alfred 11, 66, 109

Barcan Marcus, R. 158, 173
Barwise, J. 153, 169, 173
Bayart, A. 156
van Benthem, J.F.A.K. 115, 170
Berger, A. 149
Bergström, L. 115–118
Berka, K. 79
Berkeley 69
Birkoff 143
Bocheński, J.M. 85
Bolzano, B. 17, 134
Bondi, H. 89
Bonevac, D.A. 67
Bosch, P. 14n
Boyle-Mariotte 86
Burge, T. 11, 56n, 164n
Burkhardt, H. 11, 151
Butrick, H. 164

Callaway, H.G. 28n
Campbell, R. 89
Carnap, R. 19, 29, 65, 66, 86, 102, 157, 166
Carroll, L. 28
Chateaubriand, O. 95
Chihara, Ch.G. 71, 92, 95
Church, A. 68, 70, 153
Chomsky, N. 36, 72, 136, 171
Clavelin, M. 35, 106n
Cocchiarella, N. 170
Cohen, B. 21–23, 171
Condillac 44
Copernicus 55
Couturat, L. 156
Craig, W. 121

Dale, A. 130
Dalla Chiara, M.L. 143, 145
Darwin 106
Davidson, D. 48, 113
Deckert, M. 136
Degen, J.W. 93
Destouches-Fevrier, P. 144
Dewey, J. 42
Dilworth, C. 38, 125n
Ducrot, O. 167
Duhem, P. 28–30, 115
Dummett, M. 31, 34, 46, 171
Duns Scotus 163

Einstein, A. 30, 38, 124
Essler, W.K. 13

Faltz, L.M. 133
Feher, M. 119n
Feigl, H. 123
Feyerabend, P. 124
Føllesdal, D. 34, 56, 134, 155, 157, 160 170, 173
Frege, G. 35, 40, 41, 69, 94
Friedman, M. 52

Geach, P.T. 145
Gentzen, G. 140
Gibson, R.F. 13, 44
Glotzbach, Ph.A. 60, 61
Gochet, P. 41n
Gödel, K. 100
Gottlieb, D. 70
Grice, H.P. 16, 21–26, 39
Grünbaum, A. 30
Gupta, A. 91, 162, 173

Haack, R. 145
Haack, S. 11, 43n, 132, 142, 149
Hacking, I. 140
Haller, R. 41n
Hauptli, B. 111

191

Hausser, R. 11
Hazen, A. 11
Hesse, M. 37, 38
Hickman, L. 79
Hilbert, D. 15, 100
Hinman, P. 139, 172
Hintikka, J. 70, 156, 160
Hobbes 115
Holdcroft, D. 11, 59, 171
Hubien, H. 56, 61n
Hume, D. 35, 105

Kalinowski, G. 85n
Kanger, St. 156
Kaplan, D. 161, 163, 173
Katz, J. 133
Keenan, Ed. 133
Kim, J. 139, 172
Kripke, S. 156, 166, 173
Kuipers, Th. 124
Kvart, I. 166n
Kuhn, Th. 124
Küng, G. 81, 82

Ladmiral, J.R. 58
Langford, C.H. 79, 151
Largeault, J. 13
Lauener, H. 11, 13, 37, 83
Lavoisier 145
Leibniz 54, 151, 152
Lesniewski, St. 79
Lewis, C.I. 79, 151, 152, 157
Lévi-Strauss, O. 25
Lévy 90
Lévy-Bruhl, L. 25
Lindenbaum 143
Locke 35
Lorentz 124
Löwenheim-Skolem 93, 139
Lyons, J. 62

McRobbie, M. 11, 101
Menne, A. 11
Meyer, R. 101
Michelson 124
Montague, R. 133
Moore, G.E. 133
Moravcsik, J. 11, 56, 57, 59, 171
Morley 124
Mortensen, Chr. 86, 87
Mulligan, K. 113

Neurath, O. 108, 111, 112
von Neumann, J. 94, 143
Newton 38, 14
Newton-Smith, W.H. 117

Ockham 92, 123
Oosten, J. 124
Oppenheimer 103
Orenstein, A. 13, 99n

Parsons, Ch. 71
Parsons, T. 158, 173
Pascal 100
Peirce, Ch.S. 34, 35
Perry, J. 153, 169, 173
Poincare, H. 30, 117
Popper, K.R. 128
Post, H. 87
Priest, G. 26–28, 146, 171
Pseudo-Scotus 79
Ptolemy 55, 168
Putnam, H. 109, 113, 114

Richards, Th. 104
Richir, M. 125n
Ricketts, Th. 49
Rogers, R. 73
Romanos, G.D. 13, 82, 96, 97
Routley, R. 11, 101
Russell, B. 15, 41, 101, 112, 150, 152, 163
Ruytinx, J. 109
Ryle, G. 81, 134

Salmon, M.O. 162, 163
Saussure, F. de 63
Scheffler, I. 72
Sheffer, H. 101
Simons, P. 113
Schramm, A. 125n
Smart, J.J.C. 11, 88n, 107
Smith, B. 113
Sosa, E. 107
Stich, S. 139, 172
Strawson, P.F. 16, 39, 69, 135, 172
Stroll, A. 11
Stroud, B. 107, 108, 110

Tarski, A. 40, 81, 96, 114, 127, 128, 130, 171
Taylor, B. 11, 72–75, 91
Thom, P. 79
Trapp, W.R. 83–84, 171

Ullian, J.S. 33

Vaihinger, H. 104
Van Bendegem, P. 41
Veltman, F. 120
de Vries, G. 124
Vuillemin, J. 31, 76–79, 84, 171

Waragai, T. 85
Weyl, H. 115
Whitehead, A.N. 15, 101, 150, 152
Wilson, M. 116
Wittgenstein, L. 16, 109, 112, 137

Zuber, R. 24

Index of Subjects

Absolute space 124
Abstract entities 68
Abstraction: class- 78; definition by 130
Accidents of substances 84
Accidental traits versus essential traits 157
Adverbs 132–134
Agreement (principle of maximizing agreement) 146
Alethic modal logic 166
Ambiguity (lexical) 165
Analogy 104
Analytic hypotheses 51, 52, 54, 56, 147; in L_0 19; sentences 28; statements 15, 25, 27; truths 17; synthetic distinction or dichotomy 20, 21, 24, 26, 29, 35, 37, 38, 144, 148, 168; versus logical truths 126–138 passim
Analytically valid 133
Analyticity 19, 21, 24, 26, 65, 126, 133, 136
Analytique 148
Anthropomorphic hypotheses 53
Arguments 133; paradigm case 36, 109
Aristotelian essentialism 157–160, 163
Arithmetic 45, 100, 134
Arrogance response versus ignorance response 120
Ascent: metalinguistic 74, 168; semantic 67, 74, 75, 114; syntactic 75
Assumption 72
Astronomy 31, 88
Attitudes: propositional 164–168
Attributive position versus substantive position 76
Aufhebung 112
Axiomatization 100, 134
Axioms 26, 137, 143
Axioms versus rules of inference 26

Background theory 98
Bearers of truth versus meaning 82n
Behavioural coordinates 146; definition 46; semantics 34, 39
Behaviorism 42
Behavioristic reconstruction 43
Being: 66; modes of 85
Bilingual 49, 58
Bivalence 120
Boolean operations 133
Branching: possible versus unavoidable 118

Calculus, see predicate calculus; sequent 140
Canonical notation 67, 77, 170
Cardinality 94
Cartesian coordinate 88, 89
Categories: grammatical 130; ontological 67, 92, 95, 171; syntactical 79, 80, 133, 167; ultimate 67
Change of meaning 48
Charity: principle of 64, 144
Check-points 36
Chemistry 90
Circle: principle of the vicious 102
Circularity 105, 106
Class: abstraction 78; null- 139; universal 139; virtual versus real 78, 99
Classifiers 60
Coextensive 18, 35, 36, 152
Coextensivity 18
Collateral information 29, 37, 47, 48
Commitment: ontic 75; ontological 60, 61, 67–71, 85, 90, 92; primary versus secondary 75
Compartimentalization 31
Compensatory juggling 57–59
Completeness of the predicate calculus 135; theorem predicate calculus 138
Concepts: reconstruction of 102
Conceptual scheme 26; studies 100, 141
Conceptualistic theory 84
Conceptualists 171
Concretion: law of 78
Conditionals: observation 116, 122, 125

195

Confirmation 20, 125
Conflict 142
Conglomerate: language-theory 35
Connectives 147
Consequence: logical 128
Conservatism 119
Consistency 101n
Constants: logical 132, 137, 140, 143
Constructions 131, 133; *de re* 161, 165–169; doxastic 150, 164–167; epistemic 134, 167; finite number of 131; grammatical 32, 54, 56, 59, 134; modal 150
Context: hyper-intensional 169; of discovery *versus* context of justification 124 and of quotes 151
Contextual definitions 155
Contradiction 141
Convention 140; convention-T 73, 97; truth by 127, 140
Conventionalism 30, 65, 171
Coordinates, *see* behavioural coordinates 146; Cartesian 88, 89
Copula 78
Correction: theoretical 30
Correlational information 22
Correspondence: theory of truth 120, 121; rules of 124
Cosmology 89, 117
Count-noun, *see* term
Counterfactuals 113
Craigian elimination 121

Danglers: epistemological 123
Debacle: ontological 90
Decision 65
Deduction: closed under 27
Default inference 21
Definite descriptions 95
Definition 100–102; behavioural 46; contextual 155; explicit 90; recursive 97
Demonstratives 163
Denumerable *versus* indenumerable (domain) 94
Designative occurrence 151, 165
Designator: rigid 159, 166; vivid 166
De re versus *de dicto* 161, 165–169
Deviant logic 38, 141–149, 173
Diachronic 35, 38
Ding an sich 108

Disagreement: verbal *versus* in belief 36, 61
Displacement of metaphysics 90
Dispositional terms 102
Disquotation device 113
Doctrinal versus conceptual studies 100, 141
Dogma 16, 20, 26, 28, 36
Domain 73, 87, 94, 97
Doxastic constructions 150, 164–167
Duhem-Quine hypothesis 28–32, 115
Dynamics 31

Economy 94
Electrons 87
Elimination of dispositional terms 102; Craigian elimination of theoretical terms 121
Empirical equivalence of theories 114, 116; information 17; semantics 44
Empiricism 15, 20, 31, 33, 171; relative 40
Entailment 133
Enthymeme 64
Entities: abstract 68; extralinguistic 73; linguistic 73; mental 84; physical 84
Enumeration 128
Epistemology 67, 89, 100–125
Equipollent 143
Esse est percipi 69
Essential occurrences 127, 134, 137
Essentialism 157–160, 163, 167, 173
Ethnocentric predicament 53
Ethnologist 25, 45, 47, 50
Evidence 113, 172
Excluded middle: law of 141, 148
Existential generalization 151, 165, 166
Experimental method 50
Explanatory power 62, 86
Explicans 49
Exportation 166
Extension *versus* intension 61
Extensional 71, 77, 84; canonical notation 170; language *versus* intensional language 18; relation 71; semantical metalanguage 73
Extensionality: principle of 150
Extensive ontology *versus* intensive ontology 83
External questions *versus* internal questions 65
Ex vi terminorum 24, 137

196

Fallacy 20
Favouritism 157
'Fido'-Fido theory 81
Field of force 29
Field theory 87
Figurative reading 24
Finitist constraint 121
Formalism 15
Foundationalism 100, 101, 105
Framework 65; extensionalistic 173; linguistic 67; logical 144
Frequency information 22
Function: proxy 92–95, 107, 110
Functional knowledge 22
Functor logic 69

Generalization (existential) 151, 165, 166
Genericness 24
Genetic reconstruction 102–104
Geocentrism 55
Geography 88
Geology 88
Geometry: physical 30
Gradualism 28, 46
Grammar 172
Grammatical: constructions 32, 54, 56, 59, 134; rules 27; theory 136; structures 129, 130
Grammaticality 131, 136

Haecceitism 163
Hallucination 29
Hedge 23
Heliocentrism 55
Hermeneutic approach 43
Higher order logic 80
History 88
Holism 29–35, 82, 171; epistemological 34; general 137; semantic 35
Holophrastic sentences 63
Homomorphism 93, 94
Hyper-intensional contexts 169
Hyper-pythagorean monism 87, 89, 98
Hypothetico-deductive method 50, 51
Hypothesis: scientific 56

Identification 163; across moments of time 160, 162, 173; across possible worlds 160, 162, 173
Ideology 90, 91
Ignorance response *versus* arrogance 120

Ill-formedness 27
Immanence of truth 114, 172
Implication: material *versus* logical 71, 137
Impure numbers 86
Immunity, *see* provisional 146
Incommensurability: of logic 142, 143; of theories 37, 38, 124
Incompatibility: logical 123; strong 123
Indeterminacy of translation 51–57, 61, 62, 64, 95, 120, 144, 147
Indexicals 95
Indirect reference 152
Individual electrons 87
Individuation of theories 118
Induction 47, 50, 101, 105, 106, 148
Inference 26–28
Infinite regress 146
Infinite sets 84; potentially infinite class 130
Infinitives: naked 169
Infirmation 20
Information 48; collateral 29, 37, 47, 48; correlational 22; empirical 17; frequency 22
Inscrutability of reference 57–60
Instrumentalism 107, 121, 124
Intellectual intuition 15
Intension 41 n, 52
Intensional language *versus* extensional language 18
Intensional 72
Intensionalists 133
Intensionality 75, 152–154, 173
Intensive ontology *versus* extensive 83, 84, 171
Intentional predicate 72
Interchangeable *salva veritate* 18, 156
Interlocking of sentences 32
Internal questions *versus* external 65
Intertheoretic 119
Intuitionistic (logic) 140
Intuitionists 148
Involvement: modal 153, 168
Irrational elements 117
Irrevisably true 26
Isomorphism 97, 98
Judgment: of validity 27; typicality 22

Knowledge 15, 29, 100, 134, 144; functional 22

197

Language: nominalistic *versus* realistic 68; thing- *versus* sense-datum- 66; *versus* theory as far as translation is concerned 63; *versus* theory as bearers of ontological commitment 68
Language-theory: conglomerate 35; distinction 63; ordinary language theory philosophers 36
Law: Boyle-Mariotte 86; of bivalence 120; of concretion 78; of excluded middle 141, 148; of existential generalization 151, 165, 166; physical 45, 89; of universal instantiation 151; *see also* Leibniz's law
Learnability constraints 57
Learning 46, 103, 104, 171
Leibniz's law 151, 154, 157, 165, 166
Lexemes 51, 63
Lexical: ambiguity 165; items 130
Lexically 32
Lexicalization 23
Lexicon 63, 172
Lindenbaum property 143
Linguist 51
Linguistic: analysis 16; entities 73; turn 66
Löwenheim-Skolem theorem 93, 139
Logic 27; alethic modal 166; branching temporal 162; deviant 38, 140–149, 173; doxastic 150, 164–167; epistemic 134, 144; first order 93, 140; functor 69; good 27; higher order 80; intuitionistic 140; intuitionists 148; linear temporal 102; predicate 134, 135; propositional 134; quantified temporal 161; quantum 144, 145; second order 140; temporal 170; tense 170; truth of 129, 137
Logical: constants 132, 137, 140, 143; form 133; framework 144; particles 17, 128, 134, 137; pluralism 144; positivism 15; positivists 16, 109; truths 16, 17, 25, 28, 65, 126; words 15, 128

Manual of translation 58
Mapping 56, 98, 117
Mass-term *versus* count-term 54
Material implication *versus* logical implication 71, 137
Mathematical: objects 41; sequences 40
Mathematics: pure 90, 140

Maxim of minimal mutilation 141; of simplicity 123
Maximal model 158
Meaning 17, 29, 36, 41, 42, 52, 62, 81, 82, 95, 102, 136, 137, 141; conceived as an entity 39; *versus* collateral information 47; *see also* Stimulus meaning
Meaningful 15, 17, 82
Meaningfulness 158
Meaninglessness 25, 109, 110, 119, 154, 164
Mechanics 38, 170; quantum 141, 143; *see also* Newton mechanics
Metaphor: of a building 101; of the field of force 29, 32; of the house built on piles 101; of the periphery and interior 31–32, 137; of the tottering arch 101
Mentalism 39
Mentalistic semantics 41
Mentality: prelogical 25
Mention *versus* use 74
Metalanguage: semantic 66, 73, 74; syntactic 19, 66, 74
Metalinguistic 66; level 71; predicates 73, 152
Metaphorical reading 24
Metaphysical questions 66
Metaphysics 15, 16, 66, 81, 90
Method: experimental 50; hypothetico-deductive 50
Metric 30
Modal 150; constructions 150; involvement 153, 168
Mode: material *versus* formal 66; of being 85; of referring 85
Model: maximal 158; theoretic 28
Moderate realism 84, 171
Moebius strip 112
Monadism 76
Monism 76; hyperpythagorean 89
Monolingual 36
Monotonicity principle 22
Morpheme 51
Mutilation: maxim of minimal 141

Naked infinitives 169
Names 151
Natural: language 133, 136, 170; selection 105
Naturalism 42, 50, 108
Necesse per accidens 45
Neo-positivist philosophy 65

198

Neutrinos 122
Newton mechanics *versus* Notwen 117
No class theory 84
Nominalism 41, 68
Nominalistic language 68
Nominalized sentence 80
Norm 113
Normative epistemology 114
Notation 142; canonical 67, 77, 170
Notational variant 116
Notwen's mechanics *versus* Newton 117
Null class 139
Null set 88
Number theory 139
Numbers 96; impure 86

Object: language 156; mathematical 41; physical 45, 86;
Observation 29; conditionals 116, 125; predicates 102; sentences 32, 33, 44–46; statements 29, 32; *see also* Passive; Pegged observation sentences; Possible observation *versus* past, present and future observation
Occasion sentences *versus* standing sentences: *see* sentences
Occurrence: designative 151, 165; essential 127, 134, 137; vacuous 127
Ockham – maxim 92; razor 123
Ontic commitment 70
Ontological: *see* Commitment; Debacle; Reduction; Relativity
Ontology 65–67, 85–92, 97; epistemology of 98; extensive *versus* intensive 83; relative 95
Opacity 150; of quotes 75, 151, 152; referential 152, 155, 161
Operator: modal 170; temporal 170; suspending 23; suspension 23; typicality 22, 23
Order 76
Ordered pair 77, 83
Ordinary language philosophers 36

Paradigm case argument 36, 109
Paradox 73, 120; of cultural relativism 119
Particles: logical 17, 128–130, 134; physical 62
Particulars 67, 162
Passive observation 50

Pegged observation sentences 116
Perceptions 115
Perceptual similarity 44
Petitio principii 105
Phenomenological standpoint 106
Phlogiston 145
Physical object 45, 86; predicates 91; science 107
Physicalism 87, 145
Physics 29, 45; special relativity 170; theoretical 89
Physiology 29, 89
Picture theory 81
Platonism 39–41; extensional *versus* intensional 84
Platonistic semantics 41
Polyadic predicates 78
Position: attributive *versus* predicative 76; opaque *versus* transparent 152; predicative *versus* attributive 76; subject 81; transparent *versus* opaque 152, 169
Positivismus Streit 111, 172
Possible observation *versus* past, present, and future observation 115, 116, 125
Postulates 19
Pragmatism 107
Predicament: ethnocentric 53
Predicate 71, 78; calculus 73, 95, 131, 138; coextensive 152; completeness of the calculus 134, 135; logic 134, 135; metalinguistic 152; position of 78; quantification of 77, 79; reconstrual of 116–118; status of 79–83; variable 76; *versus* names 77
Predication *versus* reference 58, 77
Prelogical mentality 25
Prepositions 81, 133
Presupposed objects 69
Presupposition: existential 69
Principle of charity 64, 144; of compositionality 170; of contradiction 141; of extensionality 150; of identification 160, 162, 173; of maximizing agreement 146; of monotonicity 22; of truth-functionality 150; of verification 15, 109–111
Probability summary 21
Progress: scientific 114
Proper names 151
Properties 41n, 173; accidental 157; essential 157; Lindenbaum 143

Proposal 109
Proposition 41
Propositional attitudes 164–168; connectives 147; logic 134
Prototype 21
Provisional immunity 146
Proxy function 92–95, 107, 110
Pythagorism 93; Hyper-pythagoreanism 89

Quadratic relations 31
Qualification of the value of a variable 85
Quantification over classes and properties 82; over predicates and sentences 79; substitutional 99
Quantum mechanics 141, 143
Question: epistemological 67; external *versus* internal 65; illegitimate 111; immanent *versus* transcendent 108, 112; ontological 67, 96; philosophical 107; semantic 67
Quotation 17, 151, 165
Quotes: opacity of 75, 151, 152

Rational reconstruction 102, 103
Real classes 99
Realism 31, 68, 108, 121, 137; moderate 85; physical 89
Realistic language 68
Reality 65–67, 109, 137; general structure of 137
Receptual similarity as opposed to perceptual 44
Reconstrual of predicates 116, 117
Reconstruction: behaviouristic 49; genetic *versus* rational 102
Recursive definition 97
Reduction 95; Dedekindian 94; Fregean 94; ideological 90; von Neumann's 94; ontological 88; sentences 102, 104
Reductionism 20
Reference 39, 52, 61, 81, 82, 95; divided *versus* undivided 83; indirect 192; inscrutability of 96, 171
Referential opacity 152–154, 173; transparency 153, 165, 173
Referring: modes of 85
Regimentation 127, 170
Regimented language 136; theory 95
Regressio ad infinitum 26, 146
Relative: *see* Empiricism; Ontology

Relativism 114, 119, 120, 172; cultural 119
Relativity: ontological 95–99, 120; *see* also Physics
Response arrogance *versus* ignorance 120
Revisability of logic 145, 146
Rigid designator 159, 160
Rules of correspondance 124; of inference 26–28, 143; grammatical 27; semantical 19, 27, 75; structural 140; of translation 118

Salva congruitate 79, 130
Salva veritate 17, 18
Satisfaction: definition of 97; conditions 82
Sceptic 106; answer 109; doubt 107
Schema 138; validity of 138
Schematic 45, 72, 80
Scheme: conceptual 26
Scholastics 45
Science 15; physical 107
Scientific: hypothesis 56; progress 114; theory 36
Sectarism 123
Selection: natural 105
Self-refutation 109
Semantic: ascent 67, 74, 75, 114; metalanguage 66, 73, 175; predicate 73; questions 67; rules 19, 27, 75; structure 63; term 73
Semantics: bad 81; behavioural 34, 39; deep level of 143; empirical 44; formal 19; mentalistic 41, 42, 171; platonistic 41, 171; situation 169
Sensation 44
Sense 29
Sense-data *versus* physical objects 45, 86, 106
Sense-datum language 66
Sensory-inputs 36
Sensory stimulations 43
Sentence: eternal 45; nominalized 80; observation 31, 32, 44–46; occasion 34, 36, 44–46, 48, 50, 51; reduction 102, 104; standing 44–46, 50, 51; tensed 116; tenseless (verb) 116; theoretical 32, 44
Sequence 40, 97, 107
Sequent calculus 140
Set: infinite 84; null- 88; theory 80, 93
Sheffer-stroke 101

Similarity 131; perceptual 44; of possible worlds 113; receptual 44; standards of 105
Simplicity of a manual of translation 55, 56; of a physical theory 123, 124
Singular terms 160
Slingshot argument 153, 173
Solipsism 113
Space (absolute) 24
Speech 58
Statics 31
Stimulation 43–45
Stimulus-meaning 43–44, 47–49, 147; postulate 43, 48
Structure: grammatical 129, 130; semantic 63
Structural rules 140
Structured wholes 33, 50
Structureless wholes 33, 171
Subject-position 81
Substance 84, 85
Substantive position *versus* attributive position 76
Substituent 138
Substitution 18, 128, 139; lexical 129, 130, 139
Substitutional quantification 99
Substitutivity (principle of) 151, 154, 157
Surface syntax 59
Suspending operator 23
Suspension-operator 23
Syllogism 133
Syncategorematic 81
Synchronic-diachronic distinction 35
Synonym 17
Synonymity, synonymy 18, 25, 47, 127; interlinguistic 43; intralinguistic 42; stimulus 47
Synonymous 25, 63
Syntactic(al): ascent 75; category 79, 80, 133, 167; metalanguage 19, 66; notion 128
Synthetic *a priori:* truths 15; principle 149
Systems (formal) 96

Tautology 137, 146, 169
Taxonomy 31
Tense 170
Tense logic 170
Tenseless (verb) 45, 116

Terms: count 54; dispositional 102; distinct 122; mass 54; mathematical 150; observational 34; semantical 93; singular 160; theoretical 30, 34, 102
Texts 63
Theorem: completeness 138; incompleteness 100; Löwenheim-Skolem 93, 139
Theoremhood 96
Theory 34–38, 114–125; background 98; onceptualist 171; Darwin's 106; empirical equivalence of 116; formulation 116, 118; field 87; incommensurability of 37, 38, 124; incompatibility of 123; individuation of 118; Naturalistic theory of meaning 42; No-class 84; physical 62; picture 81; of reference *versus* theory of meaning 61, 81, 82; scientific 36, 114–118 *passim*; tandem 123; terms 30, 34, 102; tight 118; underdetermination of 114–125
Theoreticity 149
Thermodynamics 30
Thing: language 66; words 34
Tight (theory) 118
Time: branching 162; circular 117; linear 117
Topic neutrality 134, 144
Traits: accidental 157; essential 157
Transcendent: crowbar 145, 172; question 108, 110
Transcendent(al) claim 110; question 108, 110–112; philosopher 111
Transcendentalist: anti- 109
Translation 25, 61–63; indeterminacy 55–57, 147; manual of 57, 58; radical 42, 144; rules of 118
Transparency 153
True (irrevisably) 26, 131
Truth: correspondance theory of 120, 121; by convention 127, 140; definition of truth 40; functionality 150; immanent to theories 113, 114; semantic theory of 40, 96, 97; -functions as opposed to verdict-functions 147
T.U.D. 114–125, 148
Typicality: judgment 22; operator 22, 23; statement 171

Under-determination: strict 122; *versus* ontological indeterminacy 52, 55

Unified science 65
Uniformity 129, 130, 135
Universals 67
Universal instantiation 151
Univovality 135
Unsayable 112
Unstructured whole 171
Unthinkable 112
Use *versus* mention 74

Vacuous occurrence *versus* essential occurrence 127, 134, 137
Validity 28, 132, 134, 138; judgment of 27; of the schema 138; logical 27, 28, 133
Variables 70, 73, 76, 83, 88, 90, 105; values of 68

Verdict functions 147; tables 148
Verification: principle of 15, 109–111; -theory of meaning 34
Vicious circle 102
Virtual theory of classes and relations 78, 99
Vivid designators 166

Well-formedness 27
Wholes: structured – *versus* structureless 33, 171
Words: logical 15, 128; thing 34; *see* logical constants, particles
World: external 109; possible 113, 158, 160–162; third 41